794 MINI-SAGAS

MICHAEL GLOVER

SEVEN HUNDRED AND NINETY-FOUR MINI-SAGAS

Michael Glover

Copyright © Michael Glover 2023
All rights reserved.
The moral rights of the authors have been asserted.

Cover © 1889 books.
Cover painting: *To Speak of the Woe that is in the Kitchen* © Joseph Dupré
Paragaph divider designed by Freepik

www.1889books

ISBN: 978-1-915045-25-6

Other publications by Michael Glover

Poetry:

Measured Lives (1994)
Impossible Horizons (1995)
A Small Modicum of Folly (1997)
The Bead-Eyed Man (1999)
Amidst All This Debris (2001)
For the Sheer Hell of Living (2008)
Only So Much (2011)
Hypothetical May Morning (2018)
Messages to Federico (2018)
What You Do With Days (2019)
One Season in Hell (2020)
The Timely Lift-Off of the Famous Harlequin-Fish (2022)

Others:

Headlong into Pennilessness (2011)
Great Works: Encounters with Art (2016)
Playing Out in the Wireless Days (2017)
111 Places in Sheffield You Shouldn't Miss (2017)
Late Days (2018)
Neo Rauch (2019)
The Book of Extremities (2019)
Thrust (2019)
John Ruskin: an idiosyncratic dictionary (2019)
Rose Wylie (2020)
Whose? (2020)
The Trapper (2021)
Nellie's Devils and Other Stories (2022)

As editor or contributor:

Memories of Duveen Brothers (1976)
Goin' down, down, down: Matthew Ronay (2006)
Between Eagles and Pioneers: Georg Baselitz (2011)
Robert Therrien (2016)
Monique Frydman (2017)
A Garland of Poems for Christmas (2022)

for Cynthia,
who gave me this book
one Sunday morning in a Kentish garden

Foreword

Books happen in very particular ways. The idea for this one came to me one Sunday morning, in a Kentish kitchen from which you can see a magnificent outfling of a garden which falls away from the window downhill, quite steeply, until it reaches a reservoir. That garden is famous for its rare varieties of daffodil. Once a year, experts from Kew Gardens turn up to look at them, nod in wonderment, and then leave again.

Our dear, elderly hostess – as usual, she had a flower in her white hair – pulled out a book from the shelf, a large and rather flimsy looking paperback. It was breakfast time. We still had coffee on our breath and crumbs of wheaten toast between our teeth made from Kentish Cobber flour. That book looked so brown and so old and misused, though perhaps not too old. Some pages had got lost somehow. Others had detached themselves from the spine as if they no longer much cared.

She set it down in front of the microwave. *I think this will interest you*, she said. It was a teaching aid for those who wished to learn English. She herself had used it, often. What made it so unusual was the fact that it had been written and published in Poland by a teacher of English as a foreign language during the Communist years, and as I read through some of the words and phrases, it became evident to me that it was completely of its time and place in its existential bleakness and disconnectedness.

It held out no promise of hope. All the questions and all the answers seemed to lead to soul-numbing, heart-chilling dead ends. There were no conversations with warm outcomes. On the other hand, every exchange felt as if it were a story waiting to be explored more fully. Just then, and even as I read, the idea struck me that this book could contribute to the making of something else entirely. It could be the springboard for a new project, a series of compressed stories of sorts, each one consisting of a single paragraph only.

Then, still facing the closed door of the microwave, she said something else. The words seemed to drift out of her, two of them, without any context. Or perhaps there *was* a context, but in my excitement of hearing her say those words, I had let go of it altogether. *Mini-Sagas*, that's what she had added. *Mini-Sagas!* What a perfect title for a book of tiny story lines reduced to a single paragraph!

Shakespeare was sitting next to me in the waiting room, saying nothing, or definitely much less than anyone else. I knew it was he. I recognised him by the brightness of the eye, which seemed to flash from earth to heaven and back again. Don't you ever say anything? I asked, tentatively. He shook his head, firmly, meaning: no. He got out a small piece of very stiff paper from the inside pocket of his tight Elizabethan jerkin and wrote something down. As he handed it to me, he looked away at a mother dandling her toddler. It read: *I only ever write things down.* That's why the stuff is always so concentrated, I thought to myself then: *he never dribbles it away in loose talk*. I didn't try to tell him that though. I merely nodded back and left him to it.

I wish it were all as easy as this, I said to myself, carrying on writing. Writing just leads to other writing. It never stops. You don't have to bother to pause and listen back, at which point you lose your train of thought, and get needlessly angry with the world. This is perfect by comparison. You just go on doing it. It's like a dead-straight road at dawn when the sun is just coming up. So serene. So uninterrupted. So devil-may-care. All the same, I am so pleased that this train is just now arriving.

It's right at the top of the cupboard, on the uppermost shelf. I've told you that already. You don't have to ask me again. I always keep it there. It's where it belongs. It's where we always go to find it. I've told you that again and again. There's no reason at all for you to come back empty-handed, and then leave again in such a hurry, as if I were to blame for putting it there in the first place. My plan has always been to make life as easy as possible. For both of us.

I want to be a poet before everything else. I believe I may even have been born one. But I don't know how to start. I haven't even read any poems yet. I have even been told that it is good *not* to read poems first because you end up writing the poems you have just read, but in slightly different words. I wouldn't want to do that. I would only want to write my own poems. And I know what they are already, these poems, because they are written on my heart. Would you like to hear one? Or shall I write it down first if I can find the words? Given that you are such a good poet, I hope you won't tell me that they are really your words that I'd forgotten I knew. That would be terrible. That could be the end of everything.

I just like standing outside, listening to nothing much at all. When there are no voices to be heard, there are so many things left to listen to. Don't you feel that? I wouldn't want to have a conversation about it either. Is there not something very precious, and even unrepeatable, about loneliness?

I had a dream about this little husk of wheat, the smallest amongst so many, in a field. You were hiding inside it, arms straight down by your sides, doing your best not to move, doing your best not to be conspicuous. Luckily, it didn't matter whether you moved or not because the wind was blowing so fiercely that every husk of wheat in that field was in violent motion. As were you. Did I know that you were there? Of course I did! That was the whole point of the dream! You stepped out of the husk and told me that it was your birthday, and then you blushed. I don't remember what happened after that, whether we got married later. That certainly would not have been true to life, would it?

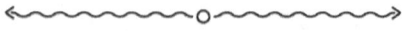

And then, all of a sudden, and for no apparent reason, everything seemed to stop happening. All the things that had happened before were no longer happening any more. How did I feel? Relief, in a way. There had always been too much of everything, too many reasons to keep opening and closing one's mouth all the time, seeking out excuses, explanations, reasons to blame even a wall for falling down and killing someone. How can a wall really be blamed for anything?

Yes, it had all got too ridiculous. So when everything stopped, and the silence of not-happening descended, I welcomed it. I wouldn't like to speak for the rest of you. There were always so few closed mouths, everywhere. Perhaps it will be a problem. Not for me though.

I always speak very directly. One word follows on behind another. No confusion. No hesitation. No love either? No human sympathy? No smiles? No hand clasps? No arm-wrestling? No light chink of glasses? No opening of doors to a stranger? No offerings of food to the needy? No sharing of the well-filled plate? I never said any of that. I am a man like any other. You must trust me.

It was a loss like any other. Whose world can we count on now? Do you have clothes you might lend me? I saw a certain look behind your look when you handed them over. Or perhaps I merely saw through to that later, when I was sleeping elsewhere. I have now pledged to eat a little less in the future, our future. I hesitated before I thought that, you know.

This is all I ever really thought of doing, sitting beside you in this chair, gently rocking. There are so many memories to be sifted, apportioned, regularised between us. We know that we are wrong when we differ. It is all a matter of time's gentleness, and of the mind's glazing over. The only difference between us, I believe, is that the sex is different, and that continues to be pleasing in its gentle, old-fashioned sort of way. There used to be so much rough-and-tumble!
Let it all happen then. I am prepared to accept this world as it comes, a portion for me, a little for you too. Even these footprints make for fairness, I believe, and the paths in this park have never been erratic. I saw a bat on your shoulder once. That was the last thing we ever needed to deal with.

Iowa, noon

There goes the wind today, said the child on the hillock, pointing, one of three, all wholesome enough, and a little simple. There stands the child on the hillock, said the second, fat and round, grinning his cheesy grin. The third one sat to the side, in the shadow of a rock, opening and closing her compasses. The entire township expects much of her, I'm told, and I may yet come to agree.

In spite of our many conversations, I still do not know what to make of myself. Sometimes my life feels too far away from me, as if I will never catch up with it, no matter how hard I try. At other times, it seems to be sitting directly on top of me, bellowing words into my ear about love, duty, good manners and healthy exercise. I find all that quite suffocating. The best thing would be for me to sit apart for a day or two, and try to settle myself into something – or someone – just a little unexpected. Why must you always open that door when I am busy talking to myself?

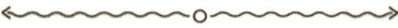

I kept it here for as long as I could remember. No one would ever dream of stealing it. It was just not interesting enough. And then things started to happen, to this town, to this region. Everything seemed to blow up all at once! You should have seen all the people, how they thronged! At first they just let it be, tiptoed around it even, made it into some kind of a public monument. Goodness knows why. It had never seemed like that to me. It's not as though anyone had actually made it with their own bare hands. To me, it had always been a thing of relative inconsequence, albeit a permanent one. There is no denying I dreamt about it from time to time. But when the tanks came straight up the middle, coughing out their filthy, grey exhaust fumes, and crushed it altogether, that was completely insupportable. I had to wipe them out and start all over again.

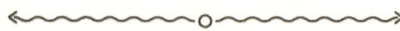

Yes and no. That's why I said it in the first place. Don't look at me like that! I'm not the only one to blame in this room. The fact is we own this field of wheat, and that's a given. Someone needs to do something about it. Talking never made the world flip over onto its back. I am only doing my best. It was you who chose me after all. And now you are all complaining that what I am proposing isn't any kind of a solution. Did you think I was a god or something? Am I not flesh and blood like you? There is no point in drifting away or shrugging your shoulders or even of harbouring general discontent. Things are as they are. The house was built. Someone sowed the grain. The wheat grew – as wheat does when the rains oblige. And now we are all standing here and looking out on it. It's practically blocking out the view! Whether or not we are completely exasperated by the situation is beside the point. A man must do what a man must do. Or someone will have to wake up a woman.

What do you mean: goodbye. It's far too soon. You only arrived yesterday evening. Don't you remember the flowers in the porch, how they seemed to greet you? Don't call me pathetic. Granted, I haven't changed very much, and that's why you say you left. The fact is though that I wouldn't know how to. And anyway, what would be the point? Who wants to become a stranger to oneself? Everyone wants to be recognised for what – or who – they are. If you stayed a little longer, I could show you that large photograph again, the one the man took of us on the bridge, when your hair blew over your eyes. You always said you loved that one. Let me see if I can find it in one of the boxes. You can sit in a different chair if you want to ring the changes. We needn't have the television on quite so loudly if that is affecting your mood. I could even look for a slightly different cheese for later. There are several. I bought several for a change, knowing you were about to arrive and stay for a little while. It's going to be a beautiful sunset. You look lovely staring out of the window. There's barely any traffic now. And I feel fairly calm.

One day I found you alone in the bedroom. You weren't even reading. It wasn't evening yet, so you wouldn't be reading. For all that, you were holding a book tight in your hand, squeezing it as if it were a lemon or something. When you saw me looking, you bounced it from knee to knee, dropped it on the floor as if it were worthless, and then left the house until Thursday. Luckily, it was one of your books. I read a lot. I even repeat words from books back over to myself when I am not reading, just after I have read them. I hear people talking a lot. That can be most unpleasant, words spoken out loud by other people. Words crafted by good writers for books are often so much more satisfying, better honed, better organised, than the loose, careless talk of casual conversation. That's why I don't talk very much, because I dread human responses. That's why I don't even bother to listen most of the time.

Yes, that was my birth name. I'm glad we don't have to say it just now. Use it often if you like. Or not at all. It is all the same to me. Sometimes it feels better to float free of a name. I often forget names, or mix one up with another. My best friend, Gordon – born Sandra – now *his* name has a certain richness to it. I like saying it out loud, though not in his presence because he is embarrassed by it. He hadn't especially wanted to be a Gordon, a Scotsman, but he couldn't make up his mind, and eventually somebody made it up for him because, as that person explained, quite gently yet forcefully, *you have to have a handle in this world*. Needless to say, I am inclined to disagree.

When you came back that first time, you were carrying far too many of the old things with you, and so I asked you to leave them outside. In the street. In the barn. Wherever you thought fit. You must be the judge of the perishability of things. And then, when I came to look at you a little later, I saw that you too had grown much larger than you had ever been in the past, and so I asked you, fairly politely in my opinion, whether you could leave a little of yourself outside too. In the street. In the barn. Wherever you thought fit. To cut a long story short, I have no idea where the best place might be for myself in the aftermath of all this prolonged argumentation. I have only ever lived in this house, with you, albeit intermittently with you. I can still see inside it, through that gap beneath the blind. You are still living in there, refining my portrait, a lifetime's endeavour. I do thank you for that. I would never unzip my mouth to call you a lousy painter.

Let me challenge you then. No one could ever stand up and solemnly accuse me of unacceptable behaviour. It would be unreasonable so to do. It would be construed as outlandish, and perhaps even indecent, I don't know. I have this suitcase here beside me for a very good reason, perhaps even for several very good reasons. I travel with it. It is my closest companion. You see, I never know when I am going to need to depend upon it again. That is why it goes with me wherever I travel. That is why it is beside my chair in this restaurant. That is why I choose to sit on it – instead of graciously accepting this chair that I have been offered again and again by a variety of waiters. To say it all over again, I do not regard this as unreasonable behaviour. It is all I have. It is everything that I depend upon. Everything else comes and goes. Even you come and go because I exasperate you so – in spite of the fact that you still insist upon describing me as your closest friend. No, it is not large enough to live inside. That would be a preposterous suggestion. What is more, the poison of facetiousness is of no help to anyone. To make it absolutely clear, in spite of the fact that it is a relatively large suitcase, I am an even larger person.

I see no reason not to write down all these poems that are swimming around in my head. They come at me at such speed. They exhilarate me. They make every new morning seem so fresh and so young! A morning in *this* place *fresh and young*? you say to me, feigning incredulity. Yes. Yes! I am not joking. Poetry has done this to me. It is a kind of lifeline or religion. I wake up thinking about it every morning, and then all at once, as if by some miracle, it springs up, gushes forth, like a never ending stream. Should I let the world know?

You recommend extreme caution. The world may not be ready for it, you advise me. Let me ask you this then: if the world has been deemed to be ready for the seventeen collections you have published over a lifetime of poetic endeavour, why would there not be space for one new book by me, albeit a fairly large one, and, yes, ever growing and growing with each bright new day oncoming?

You told me that God does not cry out in the middle of the night. He sleeps – like the rest of us. He cries out only when people are awake to hear him, so that the message will be heard. It stands to reason. And yet I heard him last night. It could have been no one but God, I told myself, as I sat by my bedside, trembling. That very particular cry of pain and exasperation was surely his. That cry of frustration that we had so comprehensively rejected him. And those bellowings of anger which followed. How could he not feel extreme anger by now? I thought to myself, knowing how long we had spent ignoring him, drinking all those slow coffees in all those cafés?

If I could transport us both there again, I feel that all would be well between us, that we would be able to speak or meet each other, that we would not now be living in different cities, separated by such an expanse of waters... I know now that this must surely be true because I returned there myself yesterday, and experienced it all over again, just as it had been for us. I bought the very same food that we had eaten together. I lit the candles that we lit, all seven of them, one for each year that we had been together. And then I walked along the coastal path a little way until the sun dipped down behind the headland, and I was obliged to return somewhat in a hurry because, o foolish man that I am, I was wearing so little.

I am bored by the need to climb such stairs as these. It is not their steepness which perturbs me. It is the very fact that they seem to throw down this small challenge to me – as if I should be caring about such a thing! I am bored by so much these days. Even my sighs disgust me. Your sidelong look bores me. Every single work of literature bores me. The sun bores me, the way it gently fingers the nape of my neck. The only thing which does not bore me is sleep. I love to be taken into the opening, beckoning arms of sleep. I could sleep forever. I wish I could sleep forever. Perhaps it is any insomniac's common wish.

There are always such prolonged opportunities for the gape of windows. They conduce to such pleasurable idleness. I would refuse all walls, and welcome all windows because they always give out onto worlds of such surprise. That surprise is not necessarily one of pleasure, but the very fact that the window comes between means the pain and the torture and the bloodshed are always conveniently distant and soundless. It is always so serenely cinematic. You are always elsewhere, behind the public privacy of your window, doing nothing but look, smile and wonder at the world, being obliged to raise not a single finger in admonition.

My friend Patience died too soon. We invited her into our home, myself, my mother, my father, all acting together as we are inclined to do, only last week. Then she grew sickly, and we were obliged to care for her. I dealt with the bandages, my mother with the spittoon. My father ground the pills into a fine powder so that she could swallow the health-giving content down without demur. Her anger was very great throughout, which sorely tried our own Patience, who lives with us too. Two Patiences in the one small, wooden house. They were obliged to live together for the briefest of brief durations. And now our own Patience lives happily beside us once again, alone, in her own tiny upstairs room, and we call on her when need be. And, needless to say, our sadness, our deep, deep sadness, has not yet gone away.

I wish I knew how to deal with the real burden of being alive. Sometimes it comes at me like a wave-surge, like a great wave-surge. There are those who endeavour to help me by encircling me from time to time — they dance around me — and even by tossing flowers on my head. This ritual of theirs distracts me, which must be a good thing. It causes me to concentrate instead upon my own sheer bewilderment. What are they doing here? How do I know them? How much will it cost me? That does help a little. I walk these uneven pavements daily. You may even have seen me. I am the one who always prepares to speak, who even hesitates on the very brink of speaking, and then does not quite speak. As I approach, you all step aside, daintily, two to the left and two to the right, as I pass through, hurriedly, like a great wave-surge.

My mother's lap did not quite fit me. Is it that I was too large for it? Is it that the lap itself was too small? When I was very young, it would cause a deal of vexation between us. I would throw over the ironing board, bellow across the field beyond the garden, and even snap the handles, one by one, off our dear ancestral porcelain cups. Could there ever be a solution to this problem? My father, being a practical mustachioed man, soon hit on the idea of a lap-extension. It would attach itself to my mother's waist by means of a circlet of metal, and then project a good metre or so into the room, surfing across her knees. Needless to say, it was fabricated from good, solid wood. I heard him working on it in the cellar, day after day, as our ugly mother-daughter stand-off continued. The first time she wore it, my mother found it so constricting that she fainted dead away. There was no alternative. I felt obligated to leave home, tender of age or not. I was a girl of some pluck. We do correspond now, fitfully. To live one's entire life as a make-weight in a nunnery has proven to be a congenial alternative of sorts.

It is the sheer monotony of life's old routines I find so difficult to cope with – morning, afternoon, evening, night. That's why I leave the light on all the time, to enforce a steady, unsleeping regularity upon my life. Who wants to be asleep and unthinking? Why so much bodily inertia? Why lie supine in a bed such as this one? That's why I try to remain standing and alert all the time. I need no props. I have prepared myself for it. I need to be an example to myself. If you passed by, you would see me standing at this window facing out to the street, were the curtains not drawn against all this fitful and undependable dark-light business. I am the one blocked out in shadow.

The train is idling here. In fact, it is just about to leave. Shall we say from Platform Three? Is it puffing out gouts of smoke like the old trains used to do? Or is that no longer acceptable in these cleaner days? Whatever. You are looking out to find me, I vainly surmise. *Oh, which platform is he on? Which exit did he leave by?* You both care and do not care to have those questions answered. Your suitcase, your ridiculously inflated suitcase, is over-full with everything you might just need, should every conceivable eventuality come into play. For two or three days. Or two or three months. Or even two or three years. No, I haven't left. Would I leave! I am still sipping from this cup of deep and wholesome coffee, watching you. My suitcase is full too, but it's not here with me. I left it at home, full of house bricks. No one carries a suitcase full of house bricks. If you had only said, even just the once, I would have emptied them all out at your feet, and built us a home to live in, by some miracle of strength and productivity of which I am not capable. Your awareness of me stretched that far, easily.

There is a place where you would always sit and listen to me, where we would listen to each other as if we had all the time in the world. It is just a little way away from here, I am quite sure of that. You only have to watch me point just beyond the window. Now it is too far away for me to travel. My legs refuse to budge from this spot. Luckily, I wrote down, day by day, week by week, everything we said to each other in those long gone and cherished days. I can sit in this chair now, reading them over to myself, all those clever words we tossed back and forth when we knew so many things and were so truly alive. I hear you say to me just as if it were now: that is not what I said. You wrote it down incorrectly. I smile at you then just as I used to smile, pretending to show you some patience, swallowing all my exasperation. That is *exactly* what you said then, I reply. You called me a coward and then you slapped me. I close my eyes and I feel the glow on my cheek, the resounding after-glow of that fierce slap of yours. We experienced such closeness then, in spite of the occasional blip.

If I had a resounding name such as Percy Bysshe Shelley, I would of course encourage you to use it. I would tell you, straight out: this is one name above all others which bounces back and forth down the centuries. I am proud to offer it to you. Feel free to say it after me. Feel free to shout it out loud. We could even shout it together if you have an appetite for such things. *I* do. I saw you try to make a shape with the words, pulling your lips about. You have small lips, and they are always so immobile. Don't bother yourself then, I said, annoyed by your pusillanimity. I can do it for you. It's not so difficult. I do not want you to do it for me, you replied, through those immobile lips of yours. They barely open when you speak to me. I do not want your mouth to be full of the usual lies about your absurd, minor role in the god-given inheritance of poetry.

I have at last laid down this unspecified burden that I have been carrying for some years. And now I am ready – and perhaps even eager – to speak to you. You too bear a burden, and you have not laid it down. It makes your back look hunched, exaggeratedly so. There is a look of extreme pain on your face. May I help you with it? I ask. May I help you to relieve you of it so that we can face each other as one at last, rid of our life-long burdens, free to know each other in a quite different way? Certainly not, you reply. It would make a nonsense, and an unseemly spectacle even, of my hunched back, were I to be relieved of this burden of mine. Everyone will feel free to say: oh look, she has a hunched back. How pitiable it is that she is so deformed.

It just didn't happen like that. You were not standing on that doorstep, looking out. I have known you all your life. You never lived in that house. You lived in this one here. I can testify to that if they ask me. And they will surely ask me because it is a matter of some gravity. Death is always a matter of some gravity – unless it happens far away from everyone else, where no one can see it and gossip about it. This death happened right here. In that house. And you were not living there then. In fact, you never lived there. And you certainly didn't die there. I can testify to that as surely as I can dip a spoon into a sugar bowl with the utmost nonchalance. And all this proves just how random and carefree all things are – in spite of every appearance to the contrary.

After I had forgotten you altogether, you became ever more real to me. I don't know how this happened. I had certainly not *willed* it to happen. But were you the person you had been back then? Were you not taller now, and a little easier to deal with on a day-to-day basis? You see, the thing is I will never know because I have so completely forgotten you that even though I might say to myself: does not that ankle and the way it twists and turns about in the back seat remind me of her, I know I can never give myself an answer which will be truly satisfying, because you have vanished like smoke from me. You have gone, utterly. And I too, I guess I must be undependable to you in a similar way in my turn, I have no doubts about that. At this moment you must be saying to yourself: I have forgotten him so comprehensively that this being who is now so real to me cannot possibly be the one I knew back then because I have no way of knowing who or what that one might have been, do I? And in this respect, we surely link hands, don't we?

All here again: the bricks with which to build. The words from which to fashion sentences. The streets to walk, back and forth. The mean and spitty rain to huddle against. The nasty clamour of human voices. Too much treacle by half for a small glass jar such as this one. Too many intemperate remarks, randomly out-flung. Pushing through, always pushing through. And then the turning aside, with quiet relief. I go for the turning aside, with quiet relief. Wouldn't *you* if you were yourself today and not someone else?

Those last few acts of reckless bravery were the difficult ones. I did so much so tearing quickly! I cut a bolt-straight seam through the enemy's ranks, and then I prised it open it a little more, pushing steadily, to left and to right of me, through my large, gritted teeth. How I pushed and I pushed! How I stared into the bulging, bloodshot, terrorised eyes of thousands as I uttered my blood-whipped guttural cries, which seemed to tear the very welkin in two! It is no wonder that I now sit here and wonder at the wonder of it all, a mere man such as myself, of physically straitened means, who had barely glanced at a breast-plate in a tailor's window before they all came together and bolted in place the sheer, clunky immensity of my all-over body armour, and how I moved with it then, so swift-gliding, betwixt and between, as if the entire task which stretched ahead of me were feather-light, and so comfortably within my means. Yes, no wonder that I sit here now, a little shrunken and diminished, a little, to say the least, exhausted by this prolonged imaginative re-enactment of it all, asking myself again and again, like some maddened, wing-sticky fly in a jar of jam, whether it all really happened to me, given whose mother's son I happen to be. Am I forever doomed to live in the shadow of that harridan? Yes I am. Yes I am!

I am Noah's Man. I have always been Noah's Man. My name is Oh! Ah!, a single word divided – and so featly completed too – by an exclamation mark. That is my adoptive name. I assumed that lightest of mantles in acknowledgment of the achievements of the master himself, how he gathered the beasts from all four corners of the round world, known and unknown, gathering them steadily, flicking his switch as he went, one by one, and then two by two, calling on others to aid him, from the great Manchurian Plains or the Gobi Desert, rough men keen of eye and sound of limb, rounding them all up and then pushing them along, by the tens and then by the thousands, bringing them all together in that slow oncoming tidal wave of such variegated animality, magnificent to be seen... What villages they trashed in their wake! And then, when he had them all there, to train the youthful circus trainers, whip-brandishers all, to persuade them all, fattipuffs and skinnifers galorious, to skip up the narrowest of narrow, long and bendy boards, up, over and whoopsadaisily into the Ark itself, popping them up and over one by one, with such tender care and roughness combined, and then arranging them in neat rows, and instructing the porters, such simple, obedient souls, to gather up all their ordure for fuel against those long and difficult winter months atop Ararat, that bleakest of most holy mountains, where all of them, animals and men, seemed to sing as one. And I, Oh!Ah!, was there too, singing along with the the rest of them, though there was no rest to speak of, with all that shuffling and stink-dropping and singing. A single syllable alone, as you may have remarked already, divides me from him. Him! Hymn! His Sacred Hymness!

Our conversations have always gone like this. I expect so little of conversations anyway. Words come and go. Where did they arrive from anyway? What's the point of putting them in their place? You have that same mildly expectant look on your face, with a little wryness superadded. Uniform: blue. Are you an air hostess again, as you were once? The uniform has expanded with you, as has the breadth of your cautious smile, which seems once again to indicate that you expect so little from all of this because words are almost bound to fail you. Or rather: words have always failed us. Why not take it personally? It increases the level of interest. I have no high expectations, you see. Words are poor things. They lie in bed all day, unstirring, eyes closed. They are usually of a sickly mien. They come at you, wheedling, small, demanding. They invited me to believe, ardently, when it was announced that you were here again. I don't know. I seldom do. The tannoy sounded so distant and so tinny. I could barely lift my suitcase on that day. Such a burden of heartaches in one small place!

That corner shop, it is seldom open. The lights – vertical, red neon strip, for the outside; white and horizontal, over-counter gliding, for the interior, offering up to us the golden glow of whisky bottles, tobacco, matches – seem to suggest otherwise. It is seldom true. No shop easily survives its own dying. I walk up there most evenings, when daylight is fading. It is the day's finest hour. It is the hour when the pulse races, when lights coming on in shop windows seem to suggest to me the beginnings of a prolonged excitement which will perhaps never end. It is then that I peek out of my front door on the high street and admire the lights in the corner shop, beckoning to me. I walk at unusual speed for a man of my age. I know already what I will say to her about her unchanging choice of three regular rolling tobaccos. She is a beautiful woman who lost her way around forty. Goodness knows what happened to her then. There was a waywardness, an incandescence to her before that. She was a genuine young woman all over just as I was a genuine young man. And then there came the flood, the robbery and the amputation, in quick succession. All changed. What did not change though were those lights of an evening, the sheer weight of their expectation. Even when they are not on, I still see them there, and I hobble forwards then at a tremendous pace, almost gathering speed all over again as I feel that catch in my throat.

Life, with its roaring, soaring mountains, and its small, peek-a-boo villages, is always difficult. I find it so, increasingly, the younger I become. And I am very young now in this amber state of frozen senility. It comes at me so fast and so hard that no dark and close-pent space between floor and underside of table is ever quite close enough to the ground to conceal me. How I cower! How I quake! My life as a stenographer of middling swagger in Phoenix, Arizona is almost completely forgotten. How did I get back here from there? Who made me what I am? Though I am small now, these village streets seem even smaller. And, and... these idly, loopy stretches of highway, which now seem to begin at my door – so much for that expensive promise of a rural fastness! – are so contemptibly brief. Some part of me – the failing part, needless to say – wants all that largeness again, the largeness of these burly arms spread wide until I touch both walls and then, with exaggerated care, draw them in again, almost, at least partially, as if to enshroud... That's a little better. That is the embodiment of patience, surely. You need give no further thought to a succession of meagre breakfasts. Just kindly close the door as you leave. I have a horror of gaping holes. I am inclined to leave all this oatmeal in my hair. Waste not, want not, Elsie.

Being a philosopher, I am inclined to leave in a hurry before the questions are answered. That is my way. It has been my way since I flung rubber with some violence across these meadows when I was scarcely more than a child. The station was demolished some years ago. There are road-planners too, but they sleep most of the day in the shadow of these cactus flowers. No one rouses them. We believe in them too whole-heartedly. I call my own life a make-weight of sorts. I carry a wad of putty in my breast pocket to deal with the smaller holes, but it is seldom moist enough before it dries again, always too quickly. There is always that gentle trickle of water from the civic fountain, alternating with blood when the clouds come louring. I wish there were more to be said about this landscape. If there were less of it, for example, and my vocabulary were a little wider, I could easily see myself getting going, and even reaching the end. As it is, I find myself stationary again. Remember: no station. No, I have not forgotten.

Walking is more than just a stone in a shoe. It is more than the lashing of a single branch against a bare lower leg when the dog runs hither and thither, always so eager to be here with you again, always so eager to be gone. Walking is a wholesome affair. You bless the clouds above, and they send down a little thin, refreshing rain to moisten the dry underlip. And then it comes on a little more fiercely, in furious, driving, vertical columns, and no hedge is quite wide or full or bendy-biddable enough to protect you from its chastening punishment. You smile through it all, feeling dampness rise up through the shoe sole and as far as the chest, where it lingers for a while to attend to the needs of the tender, pulsing heart. Always carry a single hard, dry biscuit with you as company, because the right way is never quite as certain as you told yourself upon embarkation. Fools may have spread their gold here and there. You stoop to pick it up, and as you do so you suffer a spasm of inner illumination, and perhaps you never trouble yourself to rise again after that because it is all a little too beatific down there amongst those pungent brown clods, in the company of sticks and stones speaking in their muffled parables, as they are so inclined to do.

I admire the fact that Lewis Grant knows right from wrong as surely as I know the hood of a car from its carburettor. He sits on his mother's knee every day – and now he is all of twenty-three! – speaking of the world in all its bewildering variety, and of how it troubles him. And his mother tells him, through an abundance of tears, to desist, child, desist, because my old bones are failing, and you are a man now of seventeen stone, do you not recognise that fact? It is not your bones that I need, mother, Lewis Grant tells her with an unlikely snarl playing about his ample lips – he was such a good boy once – but your words, mother, your reassuring words. My character is not yet fully formed! And then she lays out for him the appalling truth of the present moment. Her entire vocabulary of praise and blame, her once sweeping ability to describe the world in all its triumphs and its heartaches, its sins and its foibles, has now been reduced to this, son. I speak only of this driving pain in my knees, this unending pain in my knees. There is nothing else left for me any more, no apparatus of sanity or even of calm to hold me steady. I am reduced to this yowling, endlessly-rocking-back-and-forth nothing at all – even as you endeavour to pin me down with the intolerable crush of your repulsive, grotesquely inflated man/boy's body! Take your bottles of soda and your maxi sacks of potato chips and go, go, go, son! But never first tell me.

There is this much of life to be chanced upon. Only a sliver at the start. You make your way. You turn tail. You meet the same woman you had met yesterday, and she still walks as she walked then, idling, not seeming quite to know where she is going. You join her for a little gentle and prolonged conversation, probing the stars overhead maybe, how they stare down at you, and the rush of life beside you. It is all the enactment of life in a dream. The only difference these days is the way they have organised the houses these days, side by side, as if we all have things in common, and are merrily inclined to greet each other of a morning, when we meet at the door and exchange greedy and companionable glances. Yesterday they were stacked one upon another, and I knew no one, not even you. It reminded me of anyone's botched decision. And I really do mean anyone's. That could be a source of common misunderstanding.

I went down the hill at such a speed that the snow blew up into my face, and when I landed, laughing, in a heap at the bottom, I guess I knew then everything that life was inclined to tell me about recklessness and caution, and how enjoyment can lead to profound difficulties in the end for a young one empty of head such as I was in those blithe and misplaced days. Not that I have had many difficulties in my life. When I return to the house door with my sled, my father always takes it from me and examines the runners. What is wrong he makes right with his able fatherly hand. I trust my father to do that, always. He is old now, and he visits seldom. He still asks after the old sled though, and I show him the same yellowing photos that mother used to take of him turning it over and over outside the old workshop as she and I gently smiled at each other and sipped at our sarsaparilla in the winter sunlight. What is profoundly gone always seems so young and so stable.

I can't catch you out any more. You always have the word ready. Or even several words. Truth to tell, it makes for good weather between us because there are no bones of contention. I even admire the fence you threw up as if by some miracle – overnight, wasn't it? – between our adjacent properties. Until it stretched ahead between us, with those little beady searchlights atop, deftly turning as if in pre-planned motion. I had no idea at all how much we really needed such boundaries. Even as children, we could have profited by such a solid warning. I would not have blundered into you needlessly in the street. You would not have tossed eggs at me, seemingly at random. We would both have known, even as tiny children, that there was to be so much at stake between us.

I have no power to see into you. I accept that now. All I recognise are the surface values – the swoopings, the turns, the rising curves – and especially when you move in front of me, as if trying to escape me, or walk beside me, ever gaining speed. I wish I could do a little better than this. I wish I could interpret the words that spill from your mouth. I wish I could laugh along lightly with all the rest when you stand in the centre of the circle and make one of your key speeches. All I do is drift away, and then rest contented in the shadow, thinking of your dark surfaces, and of how I am inclined to look at them over and over, never really probing, never enquiring, never endeavouring, in all my stupid helplessness, to get to the heart of you.

If you announced that all the trees were to fall, all of a sudden – topple sideways, swooningly, I mean, like some *corps de ballet*, or as if some random truck had hit them – I would believe that. The way you had said it – the sheer power of your extraordinary conviction – would cause me to nod violently in affirmation. Yes, and I would go even further. I would add to your words and your outlandish gestures. I would speak of the loss of all the trees throughout the world, concluding with these chilling words: there shall be no more trees! Not in any wish to supplant you, of course. Merely to affirm, in front of one and all, how much I believe in you. You are my all to me. If this house were to fall on me, and I should perish in an instant, I know it will have been your wish for me. Why such an arbitrary punishment? I hear you all asking, tearfully. People, I have not even begun to explain the knots and the thorns and the snaggings of it all. Such a world of complications...

We married so long ago. Needless to say, my memory serves me ill. I recall lightly touching your bodice, making light of your wimple, swimming with you, back and forth, across the moat before the arrows streamed down, causing us to run to the welcoming shelter of the keep. We have been so much and so many to each other. This butter here on the table, in its dish, seems to embody your finger's touch. The way the dog rolls over onto its back, paws extended, reminds me of your endlessly forgiving nature. Even the way that this city is rising up around me on all sides puts me in mind of your terrible angers.

Loosely today of all days. And then there is all your hopelessness and helplessness to contend with. Who fashioned us in this way? Who in this world could ever have wanted it to happen like this? When you arrived with the ball of string and demanded payment immediately, I agree that there was a scene then because you were so new to me, and I had not expected such foolish and unruly demands upon my precious time. After all, I am who I have always been. You told me with such vehemence that you had learnt to play the piano yesterday, but when I saw it there in your parlour, settled like some old thing, and buffed so to gleam, I did not believe that for a single second because your stout arms fluttery-drifted in its direction with such alarming ease, and you dragged me along too – without an iota of acknowledged willingness on my part. We were simply there together, staring down at the ivories, weeping for worlds unknown and not yet revealed to us. Well, at least not to me. Such sentiments come and go – they have always behaved in this way. It is that of which my dear life consists, and pianos have never registered with me. It is entirely your decision that you stand around in the way that you do, staring down at me, judging me so harshly. I have determined to have no part of it. I am already in Morocco, amongst the other flies.

Show then a new caution! What exactly do you expect me to say? These are the dark days, the gone days. Do not underestimate our tragedy. It is still happening. I am up to my thighs in it, and you are wallowing too, somewhere over there, I believe. This is the last of my nights, I have already explained that to you. Beddy byes are over and done. Will we accustom ourselves to such incessant walking again when we could have behaved in a way that would have reminded all those church people of old-style temperance and at least even a measure of decency? God is a mystery to you too. Did I really slap you when you said that, with the palm of the hand? Was I still proving to be *that* inflexible? You know too well – you remember it all as if it were as little as one lifetime removed from here – that I was never in the same space as you, being Nefertiti's pledged man. Why do you bang on so with that drum? Do you really believe that the old crowd, those dear, gone, grey, incinerated ones, are still listening to you, that the chairs are still here, and that overarching auditorium too, beneath which we so loved to huddle after all that childish bungling was quite over and done? What has got into you? You were never like this when I had you in my pocket as a plaything, just days before you grew and grew. Nothing remains the same, not even this wallpaper which I am scraping off now with such admirable assiduity.

Even in this walking here and there, almost at random, there is so little genuine walking, by which I mean walking which really counts, walking which you can measure, the back and forth sort. You tell me that it is because the staircase has been removed. The fact is, you gently explain, hands in pockets, slouching like some unmannerly beast, that we are so profoundly in debt to everyone, not least the joiner who made it, that old man who died long ago, of extreme poverty, you needle me. I have challenged them though. I have asked them all to prove that they are indeed his heirs, but the entire team has just breezed past me, as if they knew who I was, and exactly where I lived, and possessed, as though centred from within like a cleric, a blade-like assurance about the nature and the importance and the urgency of their task – which was, of course, to remove the staircase, which I, needless to say, given that the morning hour is freshly upon us, was just about to mount on the way to the bedroom and my heaving wardrobe of fine clothes. What does it profit any man to be naked when other arrangements could be put in place? I cannot get to grips with any of this. It is always too much for me. There is such impertinence in this world these days. And you do not help much. When I invite you to speak, you remain locked into your sullen silence. When I ask you to hush your mouth, you blurt out like a huge dog whose tail has just been stepped on. Must I then take the left at the next roundabout? Would it help at all if I said please?

Who invited me to God's finest feast? Who even warned me that such a thing was about to happen? No one. I was chewing my nails on this forecourt, as I have been doing since the nature of time was invented, considering once again how all these statistics might add up, and what it might all amount to in the end, were there to be an ending. Should I absent myself for a little while? Should I be encouraging myself, at my time of life (which could, for all I know, be a propitious one), to move along with even greater celerity? The questions stack up like boxes in the garage. I am barely even conscious to myself any more. The weeds never seem to loosen their grip. The questions pile up. If perhaps, at a certain point in my life, when I was at my usual hopeless bath-wallowing in front of the raging fire, you had intervened decisively by pulling the plug and shouting at me decisively, and then flung the waters of truth full into my face, my anxieties might just have counted for a little less. I doubt it though. Our friendship was held in place by such a fragile length of string, which threatened to break at any moment. In fact, it finally did break because I took the scissors to it, the household scissors, I seem to recall. There are no other scissors. We are not a rich family. Not since the 16th century. I am still inclined to live in those bygone days of past magnificence.

It is a horse race. That is the designation. You stand well back in order not to be liberally sprayed – hair, coat, ears and all – with horse manure, and in order not to be trampled to the ground because, as I have just explained to you, it is an occasion which lacks mercy. I did not determine the rules. They were determined long ago, when princes went on horseback and we, we, we walked as usual, dragging our feet, muttering oaths over to ourselves *sotto voce* and, generally speaking, trying not even to see all the ignominy. And so it is now. You cannot fling yourself out there and demand the use of a stallion in order to gallop along with all the rest. You have no training. Your voice, raucously emphatic though it may be, is no species of training. You have no adroitness in the saddle. To monkey-squat and bouncy-bounce just so in front of me is proof of nothing. I brought you here for the spectacle alone. It is a form of mass entertainment in so far as it will be televised on one of the pay channels this evening. In fact, it is entertainment for the few (and virtual entertainment for the many) because there are relatively few of us here. That is why I encouraged you to fling your fox fur about your neck and to polish up your long black boots. No, you cannot leave this enclosure at whim or at a run again. If you do so, they will all bear down on you again as they did last time. And they will not merely carry you, swinging you between them, grim enough of demeanour, next time. They will fling you at me as one might fling a bucket of horse manure. And I will be left with all the embarrassment of having to scrape you up from the floor.

Perhaps your peacefulness is a little like my peacefulness. It comes and it goes at a moment's notice, when the ragings recede. I do not prefer the ragings – in spite of the fact that my entire being seems to embrace them like a long-lost friend. Those ragings remind me of how the sea comes and goes. Positively undeniable. Completely unanswerable and unstoppable. Faintly delicious in their way. You remember those quieter moments then, hole-in-corner? That's how I used to describe them. It was all such a contrived affair, I believe, with the window painted in, facing the field. I leant out from it. I even began to breathe a little. A little better, that is. In fact, my very best in-and-out breathings, so rhythmically perfect in their way. Your presence was the faintest of faint pencil drawings, done a little later. I had closed the window by then because I could already hear, in the distance, that upcoming roaring. I knew that I would hear it more and more and more were I not to close the window. I knew also that such a heartfelt and emphatic closure would be nothing but a temporary measure because within minutes – if not seconds – it would be inside here, beside me, within me. Yes, it would have engulfed me. And in order to stave this off for a little while, I would hurry away then, and try to represent what I had seen and felt of you out there, so tidy of limb, so small, so dainty, in pencil only, merely a passing breath of a being such as yourself out there, and moving along enveloped in such silence...

I say: let it all go. Why cling on? Why be interrupted by such vulgarity when there is a certain suaveness everywhere which you would be such a damnable fool not to emulate? At the first instance of knowing all of this, I wanted to keep it entirely to myself, and so I continued to fit domestic boilers on a daily basis, house after house, at such a cost to my physique, even when the young did all the heavy lifting, and thus, at a stroke, deprived me of my profit. The young, in the end, proved to be my son, of course. No other would serve me at whim. I had to wait years until he achieved the correct level of muscle. Many a day I would found myself standing and grinding my teeth over his cradle, feeling my own musculature ache and ache, asking myself: how long, good lord, how long? Needless to say, he had no wish to join me as an apprentice. His passion was to raise the violin to shoulder height, fling back his hair like some handsome wanton, and then to play and to play – before an eager mirror-audience of one, needless to say. Is a violin to be judged, in the scale of importance, beside a domestic boiler? I leave that question hanging in the air. I leave that pesky violin to play itself, like a gnat screeching on in my inner ear.

There are two or three. There is never merely the one. There is always at least one other to be nudged at and then spoken to, almost certainly interrupted. The two or three seldom know each other and seldom want to either. They are at different bus stops, on the same side of the road, within yards of each other, and each one equally impatient. Each one is thinking to himself: if I were not here, he would be here in my stead, standing in this space, eating my food with relish, testing out the credibility of my words, always so carefully chosen.

Question after question. Do things happen in this way? Is that why you walked out on me yesterday when I was in mid-sentence, addressing you? At least the lakes are cool to drive beside, and a certain inner flow takes hold, of ease and letting go. Which is what we all need these days. Needless to say, the earthquake was terrible, the way that the ceiling bounced up and down above our heads, as we circled and circled the pool. I had never heard such screaming. It is a wonder that we survived at all, those of us who did survive, that is. Not many. Half of me survived, I have to tell you, the left side. Then there came a certain inner blankness, which went on for years. I walked the same corridor, again and again, as a mere child, the child I may have been. I am not even sure about that any more. I do not recognise any of the photographs, the ones with the quizzical smile in particular, the way that the boy kept looking and looking into the camera as if all that silence would amount to meaning in the end, comprehensively. Who would not have wanted that? I had no will to will it then, and now all I seem to do is to come and go hereabouts, asking the same old questions, or others very like them. I go to address myself, hoping that it might be you again who has walked in to take an interest in what is going on around here. But it is not you, and even if it had been you, there would have been nothing for you here. The very sight of me would have caused you to shrug in the usual way, and to walk away. There is only this one again, I would have heard you muttering into your lamb's wool sleeve, and his pitiful catalogue of vain excuses.

There is no electricity out here. I am too high and too far. It is a mere cabin, out in the woods, with the winds and the couch grass leaning and leaning at ever more improbable angles, even as I stare down at it from this makeshift window, hour after hour. What else though? Oh yes, I have an addiction to the old style of telephone, black and heavy, with a dial that moves in a turning circle with the aid of the finger, and then re-settles itself back to where it began when you let it go. I lift the mouth piece to my own mouth again and again, feeling my breath warm against these parched lips, and let the part which encloses my ear fit snugly into its appointed place too. Then I feel myself ready for any and all conversations. There are no conversations. There can be no conversations. I know that very well because the telephone is not connected. It has never been connected. It could not possibly be connected out here. Who would come and do the work for me? No one. Not even the greatest fool in the world. I know that very well. I am a fool myself to dream otherwise. And yet I do dream, daily, hour after compelling hour. I dream, and I hope that when I raise it again, he will be there for me, answering all my enquiries, the greatest and the least. I must ask him so many things when I begin to speak to him, and some part of me knows full well that this precious conversation may yet begin because so much of me is inclined to *will* it to begin. Not yet perhaps, but soon. Why otherwise would I keep this telephone here beside me, looking so black and so gleaming, as if it were the latest marvel? The moment will come, I tell myself, when I have the confidence to believe that all these questions that I have prepared on these many, many sheets of foolscap paper which live, heaped up so precariously, beside the telephone – there are so many of them! – will not only be asked, but will also be answered. In the fulness of time. It is merely a question of waiting for the optimum moment, and only I can decide upon the timing of that moment. And I have every confidence that it will happen by and by, when the winds have settled a little, and the couch grass is once more standing proud, as it used to when my mother walked with me in these parts, in those days before the great sorrowing began.

⬱〰〰〰o〰〰〰⤳

It was always a small town. We liked that fact. It made sense. It felt wholly at one with our small and settled and pacific natures. We had no wish to be overwhelmed by everything that we had made. When we stared at all those pictures of tall buildings looming over, we would cry out and run to our beds and lie there in silence for hours at a time. Later we would sip at a little tea, and see to our gardens, our very small plots, saying so little to each other, remembering the shadows of those buildings looming over. And then perhaps in the evening we would read a book, one seated cross-legged beside another, lips barely moving as our eyes passed over the words of consolation. Our books consisted almost entirely of words of consolation because we all believed ourselves to be on a steady road of recovery from some terrible collective calamity, fortunate to be here, with limbs and eyes and hands intact, working, and then working a little more, albeit cautiously, digging and delving, as if it would be foolish in the extreme – and our goal was to avoid all moments of extremity – to hazard too much. And so when we talked, our words were hushed and gently enquiring, after each other's health for example, always knowing not to go too far, not to pry or to needle or to taunt. There had been in the old days one man in particular who had taunted us all, who had railed against us for the hollowness and the emptiness and the foolishness of our lives. We had settled ourselves helpless, cross-legged, at his feet, heads bowed, in a half circle, listening to the hammer blows of his words. Weeks into this torment, one of us had presumed to ask why we were still seated there, listening to his words of condemnation. We all looked puzzled, ashamed. The moment of action has arrived, this brave soul whispered to us then, as if it might have been an afterthought. And we nodded gravely, each and every one of us, because we knew that he was right. But who would act on our behalf to rid us of this pestilence? We all stared at him. He knew himself to be the chosen one. He had hazarded to speak for us. It was he who would do it. But what would become of him after the deed was done? There was no place fit to conceal him. He stank to high heaven from the burden of it all. He found the matches, the twigs, the few stout tree limbs, and he left us. We saw the smoke rising, waveringly, as the breeze caught hold of it, in the distance. We were at rest again. And we have been at rest since that moment. Yes, all is so profoundly still now. If not somnolent.

Dear Oldster. There is no such thing as the bounce and the joyous uprearingness of youth. When you are very young – as I was once – you are already bowed over with this burden of apprehensiveness, the sheer terror of the aftermath of that tragic bursting forth from the womb. Here are just a few of the problems just a few years in. Whether the milk will arrive in time to give a pale veneer to the swirling blackness of the breakfast tea. Whether the bus, coughing gouts of filth, will arrive in time to take you to the knee-scraping schoolyard at windy hill's top. Whether your strength will be equal to the task of vaulting over the giant-legged horse with the leather seat in the gym when you feel so weak and so squeamish with your jangle of stick limbs. Yes, it was so much worse back then, remember, because you were so small and so awkward and so vulnerable in your short pants, with your stuttering words and your bashful sideways glances. And at the very moment, remember, when you were expected to matter – or, at the very least, to be on the foothills of mattering. Now you possess the full freedom to be wholly ignored, to be nothing for everyone, required now merely to lean back against a wall as your hair, in all its untidy wispyness, gets blown up and about, and your stick clatters to the uneven ground from your hand. You do not need to move. You need say nothing to anyone. Even when the vulgar taunt you, feel safe to ignore them because you are of no consequence whatsoever in their lives. Even as they pass you by, they have already forgotten you. May the joy of all this forgetfulness, theirs and yours, overwhelm you.

Who was I anyway? The moment of interrogation had arrived. And, no longer fearful, I felt myself to be its equal. I set everything that mattered to me aside. It was all so much stuff, the stuff of all that I had probably misremembered. All the books went too, heaped up outside the door, inviting even a little gentle rain to rain down upon them, just as if I had never cared for them – those books upon which I had lavished so much love and attention! Had I remembered even so much as a word? Were there any little things at all left to reassure me? Had I then cared for nothing? Was everything to fly from me with the careless delight of a fledgling? Then I remembered the little black rag that had fluttered like a pennant in the yard, and I battened down on it in memory. Memory was all that remained of it, of course. Who would keep a black rag as though it were a precious object? I stared at it then, hard and long, and as I did so, I saw it proceeding in front me as if in the vanguard of some great army. Opposing troops, entire phalanxes of them, fell back, awe-struck and terrorised, as it came on, my black pennant, my beauteous darling, fluttering forever in memory, on the washing line, strung out, wall to dustbin, in our back yard.

Take back everything you ever said, every last word of it. Only in that way will cleanliness come, a new beginning, a new soul, if not a new man. Is that not what you wanted? Is that not what you always discussed with me, raving in your corner as I sat beside you, always so casually amused by your antics? And yet you were right, I do see that now. You, in all your folly – as I wrongly supposed – were right to think as you did. It was I who wronged you, and I apologise to the ghost of you for having been so wrong, for having taunted you in the way that I did, until you snatched up the spade and ran with it, with me running after, perhaps half guessing what you were about to do then because your temper seemed so uncontrollable. I also knew by then that there was nothing I could do to appease you, and, if truth be known, I was quite proud to have been able to exercise such power over you. I had never known myself to be a strong man until I met you, being such a physical weakling. I had always been such a victim, and so many, I recall it now so clearly, had taken such pleasure in victimising me because I was always so small and so helpless. Until I met you, and I recognised what power the least of my words had over you. My least touch would cause you to wheel around to face me, mouth agape with expectancy. I would always take it quite slowly. There was really no need to hurry. You would hang on my every word as if each one were a great weight dropped directly down upon your skull from a great height. And then the end came at last on the day of your running. When you reached the spot, you began to dig, dig, dig in such frenzy. Little by little you sunk, until the ever greater hole that you were digging, a hole designed, in the end, to conceal you, wholly, worked its magic upon you. You were gone. And there was silence. No, not quite silence because I could hear a small and distant mewing. I crept over. I peered over the edge to find you. Your eyes – it was only your eyes that I could see now – were pleading with me to do something for you, to make the sacrifice of you complete, to help you be done with you. I went at it with some vigour, spade after spade heaped over you, until the ground was entirely level again, and I felt able at last to leave you.

The longer I spend walking this room, the more its shape has proven to be flexible in the extreme, which has pleased me greatly. I spent so little on it, you see, because it was designated a box room when I bought it. My single bed was almost enough to fill it. I would eat on my bed – sandwiches only, bought in – because there were no cooking facilities. And then I discovered this small walking route back and forth, between the side of the bed and the wall, and I began to walk it, and as I did so, I began to talk loudly, like a man of means, or even a man of property, pushing out to the left with my elbow as I went, grazing the wall as I went. And, lo, when I turned and went back the way that I had come, there seemed to be a little more space between me and the wall. I found that I had to reach out a little – with my right hand now because I was moving in an entirely different direction – to touch it, and its length seemed a little greater too because the door, when I looked it carefully, seemed a little smaller and further away than it had been... So I tried a slightly different experiment. Instead of walking beside the bed, back and forth, I stood side-on to it, with my legs pressed back against it, and I walked forward – just a single small step because there was so little space between me and the wall. I knew that very well, of course – no cooking facilities, remember. Then I turned on my heel, and I found that I could take two steps back to the bed. Two, gadzooks! The experiments continued apace, needless to say, from bed to wall, stepping back and forth, and those slightly different ones taken in parallel with the bed. It required such patience, such determination, so many hundreds of sleepless hours of dedicated walking. And yet it has all proven so efficacious in the end, I am delighted to report. I now have several rooms, each one with a picture window, and a spacious garden in which to cartwheel and frolic and dance to my heart's content. And – who knows? - one of these days I may even meet someone with whom to share this boundless contentment, which enwraps me these days like the coarse fleece of a ram gently butting against my thigh.

Winter oncoming. My fears of the merciless creep of the boundless cold, and of the bareness of the trees, and of all those huddling figures, bent over, shivering, moving so quickly in order merely to stay alive at all. There are always such stirrings of wickedness and illegality when the winter comes on, the theft of provisions from an outlying shed, the bundling away, at dawn, of logs from the neighbour's wood pile. You hear the dull, quick, muffled snap of a gunshot. You peek out the frosted window, having cleared a small circle with your elbow, and there it is, laid out before you, the consuming horror of it all: broken body splayed out on the snow face down, spatterings of blood, stark red against pure white, and, out-flung in all directions, logs, logs, logs, as if thrown in some futile game of chance. And even then there will be many – not me though – who run out and snatch and bitch and fight for the precious contraband. Shameless! Winter is always so shameless. And where am I in all of this? I repair to the kitchen table during the few mean day-light hours and, fists bunched, eyes tight shut, I mutter the same prayers over and over, that the Great Mother will return to us, she of the mighty legs and the heaving hams, bearing on her back sacks of offal and meatstuffs, enough and overflowing for the few that we are. But does she come? Does she come before spring comes slouching slow to the rescue of the few who remain?

She was a woman I knew. Not well. A bibulous woman who would vomit in the road at weekends. That's how she got her few meagre pleasures. By vomiting in the road at weekends. Rather in the road, where many wet car wheels could disperse it little by little, than on the pavement or on a doorstep, that's what I'd say when challenged by the hot-bloods, the churchy, starch-collared kind. Always inclined to show a little clemency from time to time, being a somewhat bibulous man myself when the mood took me of a Friday evening, that night of the great letting go. We would even go arm in arm when the mood seized hold, not to talk at all – neither of us were great talkers – but for the mutual support we could give each other. The gift of remaining standing, that's what was on offer, and we were glad of it when it happened, how, through all that violent lurching, we could somehow prevent each other falling to the ground altogether, and doing our faces some terrible, horrible mischief. Blood everywhere, streaming, gushing from nose and mouth. Seldom happened. Never spoke of it later even if it did. It was as if it had never happened at all, later. I would return to my work at the post office, low-whistling through my teeth as I flung the parcels up garden, and she, of a Thursday as I recall, leaning out from her upstairs window, cleaning and polishing the gleaming leaves of her aspidistra plant. Beloved sauce, she cared for nothing else quite so much, bless her.

<----~~~~~o~~~~~---->

In the meantime, I kept on saying it as if it were an abiding obsession or something (as it was), there is nothing but *this* to attend to. It is all we have and are likely to have for the foreseeable future. Think on now when I tell you. Don't behave like brainless beasts. I had such an anger within me! And so I shoved it forward, across the table top, quite roughly. It took quite some doing. It was heavier than I remembered, and bigger too, swollen even. I remembered it as a small thing. It must have grown and grown then... They all looked on, some disinterested, others rapt, yet others with eyes closed as if they were still sleeping. Sleeping standing up, I ask you. It was all wrapped up, swathed by layer upon layer of this, that and the other – bits of blanket, cardboard, even half a cardigan. Every last thing had been snatched at, pressed into service, because we all knew that it had to be protected above all things else. How long had it been like this? How long since anyone had felt desperate enough to drag it out of the cupboard as we had just now done? The stories, I believe, went back at least three generations, how and why they had done it in the first place, what good it would all do us, why it was so necessary to our lives, to our very sense of being in this pitiable world that we inhabited in spite of ourselves. All that sort of stuff. Go on then! they were muttering at the back. Typical! I shouted out, whirling round, fists flying in all directions – they all drew back in terror. It is so bloody typical that you should expect *me* to do it, and for *you* to be hanging back, as far away from the action as possible. Who then will be the first to suffer if it all goes wrong? You will, said little Edmund, small-voiced, dead-pan, solemn as usual. Such a wry little fellow. Barely reaches as high as my mid-riff. Entirely fearless though. His head was all a-bob at my elbow. I have time for that man. I would give him space if the entire world were to fall about my ears. Quite right, Edmund, I told him, fondly tweaking his right lobe.

<----~~~~~o~~~~~---->

It stands to reason, does it not? A road is as long as you make it. It can just go on and on and on if you push it forward. The machinery these days is so efficient, overwhelmingly, overbearingly so. What is more, when you make another road, folks, the impatient, emboldened, dissatisfied sort, are always inclined to fill it, heaving and shoving and pushing along with everything they have about their persons, all else gone, blasted. It is horrible to see it. I would get rid of them all. They are too much of a menace. The idea of home is lost for ever when it is so easy to skip away from it. If there were no roads, there would be no routes to travel. They would all have to stay put. There would be no alternative to staying in one spot, making the best of a terrible bargain. And, I agree, life is a terrible bargain more often than not. Inclines would be too treacherous, mountains too mountainous by far, rivers uncrossable. Just imagine the condition of human feet if there were no roads, how torn and ragged and twisted and bloody and swelling they would be from all the jaggings and the lumpings and the spikings underfoot. It is all this smoothness and soon-to-be-getting-on-elsewhere that has done for us. When I get down on my hands and knees – as I so often do – and sweep out and around and across with my hand, I feel how easy it must be to pass along – such evenness, such flatness, such fleetness enabling.

And then the maker laid his hand upon me, his large, rough hand. I felt him do it. I was staring up into the sky, thinking nothing, feeling nothing, knowing nothing, practically asleep-when-waking, when he did it. And I did not resent it at all. So few have ever touched me. I am not pleasant to touch. I am not pleasant to smell. I am not pleasant to look at. I stand apart, quite deliberately, and often even apart from myself, proudly, knowing myself to be unique, knowing myself capable of speaking in a language known only to myself. It keeps me safeguarded, preserved as if in aspic, to know such things of myself, to commune with myself in this way, in silence and then out loud, in my own particular language. I am almost monumental, stone-like, such is the extent of my unbiddability. And I stand out in the rain regularly, calling it down upon my head, my flat and ugly head. I welcome a little gentle sluicing. I jut out my lip to welcome it in, let it trickle down my throat, as if my throat were a handy length of purpose-built guttering. Down it goes and I am satisfied. Is there anything odd about any of this, anything about this to which you might feel inclined to take exception? Evidently not. My proof is that he has put his rough and infinitely generous hand upon me. He has anointed me by that touch. He has singled me out for especial attention. When he did that, I asked him what I could do for him. I spoke the words in my own particular language and he understood me. I know that because the grasses bent in a very particular way, almost exaggeratedly, when I inclined my face upwards towards him. I knew that he had heard me and that, by and by, he would respond to me in a way that only he and I would ever understand.

When the piano strains to make its mark, when it rises up from the floor, black and gleaming, as if by some prestidigitatory power, flinging up, within seconds, its mighty shark's fin of handsomeness out of all that silence so long brooding in the concert hall, and then reminds us, so plangently, with that light-struck first chord, of its forcefulness and its beauty, it is at such a time as this that I yearn to be a small, tinkling spinet, a forerunner, as if in homage of sorts, as if in recognition of what would soon come after, and of how it would supersede me, making me so small and so grateful for having been what I then was towards the tail end of the eighteenth century. A spinet is as much and more than I would ever need or require of myself, I confess that to you without fear or favour. It is womanly, and of the utmost feline delicacy. It sits side-on against a wall, as if not expecting to command too much space, as if grateful to be owning all that it is and has. It is pale of hue, and when it speaks to us, it comes at us thinly and tentatively, every note quite scrupulously separate from every other, so sweet and so wheedlingly gracious in its attentions, requiring nothing of us but bottle-green, dandified frock-coat, high-piled, well powdered wig, lorgnette, long lace cuffs, and a voracious, full-mouthed simper.

We were away from this spot we call home for months together. We needed to travel that far, to ease ourselves out of ourselves for the duration of that punishing journey. We knew that by so doing, something extraordinary would happen inside ourselves, that by the end we would no longer recognise what we once had been. Our methods too had to be uncustomary. There had to be challenges barely known or even glimpsed by the rest of humankind. Could we do it? Would we? How though? You had the first inkling. You brought the first length of rope to me, scavenged from some outbuilding by the abandoned dock yard. We held it between us, pulled on it until it was taut. That would do. We were on our way to a solution. Then I found various rude, shapeless blocks of wood, off-cuts from the joiner's shop at the street corner, of a certain shape and age, and also several bricks, and gaffer tape with which to bind them. We set to at once, in such a mood of eagerness, if not delirium. We helped each other. Neither of us could have done this alone. It was a collective endeavour. It was some kind of recognition of our mutual regard, almost akin to love, had that word not been so perverted by ill usage. On and on we went, working through the night in the outhouse, when all the others were asleep and dreaming of those long gone days of innocence. I found a fragment of fishing net and filled it with bricks which I attached to your knee, the right one. You countered with blocks of wood in a sack, slung around my neck, so that my head felt so heavy and so lolling that it almost touched the ground. And so we added this and that, everything heavy, everything impossibly burdensome. The last to be attached were old bibles, several tied together, to the finger ends. We tried it. We did our best to move ahead. We were such heroes then! There was such a look of triumph in our faces! I knew that for sure. My spirit had grasped hold of that truth. I could not even raise my eyes to see you. All I could hear were the wails and the grunts as we both strove to heave the impossible burden of ourselves ahead, inch by inch. Would we ever reach street's end? It seemed most unlikely.

There were several men in that room, and they were talking together as if they had all the time in the world to share the most minute particularities of their wholly useless lives. I experienced such a spasm of exasperation as I listened to their every word. Why use two words when one might have done? Why talk about matters of such drooling inconsequence when such words as Particle Physics had not yet even been proposed as a topic of urgent enquiry? Why were these men, these abject clutterings of uselessness, frittering their lives away in front of this window? And what a window it was, with such a prospect of finely shaped topiary flung out in all directions across such royal parkland! My favourite was the giraffe, and in order to divert myself from the futility of all this idle listening, I found myself sitting astride it in the mind's eye, gently coaxing it along, urging it to proceed just as far as the elephant's trunk and no further. It had never been given such delightful instructions. It had not even believed until then that it possessed the capacity to move at another's bidding! Understanding quite how puzzled it was, we paused so that I could talk to it about the nature of life, and of how topiary life does not necessarily exclude the possibility of movement, provided of course that the appropriate *whispered urgings* are put in their place. This is all that is required, I told the giraffe, the urgings of a kindly helpmate such as myself, urgings of the kind to which you have just been so pleasingly attentive. Thank you.

<hr>

Mirror life never goes away. It does not know how to. It holds you spell-bound forever. There will be no end to its enthralling investigations. How in the world could there ever be because the nature of the looking will always be different, minute by minute, second by second? We go to find ourselves again, and once again we have slipped away, disappeared down that convenient side-alley. It was, after all, to be a quite separate assignation. You knew that all along, of course. It was just that you did not tell yourself. You did not dare tell what you knew already. You did not dare to hope. But what if the mirror were to shatter? What if you were to shatter it and walk away, be done with it all? Impossible! You are such a fool! A mirror has the capacity to reconstitute itself in all kinds of ways. You walk away only to find yourself again, only to be yearning to find yourself again, in another man's eyes. You are looking at yourself again even as he is looking at you, unmistakenly alive again, unmistakenly inquisitive. Whose mirror-life is haunting you today? Are you never to be seen as you really are? Questions, such vexing questions!

Let us level it then. Let us call a truce. I no longer have the patience to assail you as I once used to. The strength has all drained away from this once powerful arm. All my weaponry has rusted over the years. I am too weak to raise a sword any longer. My hair is too long, too thin, too lank, too devil-may-care. These days, my old antagonist, I prefer to stare up at the topmost branches of trees. And you too, you are too old to care, though you may wish to deny it for old time's sake, and even to rise up again, arms flailing, knees knocking, like the fool that you have always been. Truce, brother, truce then! We are too old and too frail and too far gone for such things. We have rehearsed all the arguments, again and again. We have both at last agreed on the height of the fence that must rise between us, how high it must soar, and we have also agreed – have we not? – that the colour after all must be green. Green is unexceptionable, is it not? It is the colour of harmony and earth-healing, is it not? It is the hue of bile. And it also contains, I recognise as I stare down at it now, so slow and so treacly in this tin, just a taint of an old and abiding envy.

There is talk of nothing but boxes, boxes, and I must join in because when any other matter is raised, the entire room falls silent, and I draw down a general embarrassment, heavy as any moth-eaten cloak, about my person, which I must seek to avoid at all cost. So boxes it is then. I must find ways to speak of them then, dancing ways, beguiling ways, ways which others have not even begun to guess at, in order that I may rise, as if by some miracle, to the top of the pile. Of boxes, my friend! So I speak of piling them up to the sky and, leaning from the topmost box of them all, washing the stars with a wand of my own devising, which sets them squeaking and squealing and falling about. They congratulate me. They fill boxes with gifts, and yet more boxes. Our houses are boxes needless to say. I had no need even to tell you that! Our very souls are boxes.

<hr>

As I just said, there is a certain way in which the street takes a bend half way along its length which always gives pause for thought to one and all. We have all agreed to stand there together on a Sunday and look and wonder. You see, there was no reason for anything of this kind to have happened. In every other respect, every twist and turn or turnabout has been removed from our lives, as if by means of the most delicate of surgery. We have long believed only in proceeding ahead, in a straight line, never once doubting that this is the only direction in which happiness lies. All beds on the curve have been burnt. We are all straight up and down too, never side to side, never twisty-turny. There was much opposition to this at first, indeed many lives were lost. Much raucousness and unruliness had to be expunged. It was then that I called out, so forcefully, during our street meetings. Do you not recognise, I shouted, that all this is of a piece, that unrest is at one with unstraightness, that if we were all to agree to walk ahead and only ahead, all would be well with us, that we would almost automatically usher in a new world of harmoniousness and truth and beauty? We stared at each other then. Our miserable faces looked so taut, so crabbed, so vengeful. We knew, all of us just then, that there must surely be another way. And so there was. You came to agree with me. We all agreed with each other. And we took it. Yet now, only today, we have discovered this remnant of old evils, the way a random street on the outer edge of town has taken a long, strange bend, as if in defiance of all that to which we had once pledged ourselves. Who could have fashioned it in this way? Who could have struck such an ear-grating note of defiance after years of such dreamless peace? What did we do? After days of rumination, yes, we have decided to leave it like this. It is perhaps even good for us so to do. Let us describe it as a warning of sorts, an indication of all the punishments which might have been meted out to us, and which might yet come thundering down upon us like rocks from a distant mountain.

Listen to me now. Lay down that pencil. Nothing must change ever again. That is the only way forward, to read the same books, see the same faces, open the same doors onto the same prospect of morning, noon or evening. That evenness, that steadfastness, that steadiness, will be so agreeable to us, I know that for a fact. We have wanted nothing to be different for so long. I know that as well as I know how to drive a nail into a stubby length of rough board. When I caught your lingering smile that day, playing so delicately and so persistently in my direction, I knew at once that things had to stay that way. I did not want a return to any of the old mistrust or disaffection. I wanted your smile to stay frozen like that, forever playing about my face, which necessarily relaxes and glows and even shines with goodness when I see what you are doing for me, how you are pleasing me and encouraging me and even loving me in your own quiet way. And similarly I wish only to read and to re-read various gentle works of exhortation, books and tracts which express approval that I am conducting my life in a way which is conducive to general happiness. I want all this to be smeared abroad forever like the soft melt of butter on a white ceramic platter left out all the livelong day in the sunshine, how it spreads and puddles in all the rich abundance of its yellowness. This way there will be nothing but relaxation and even a species of bright-shiningness akin to some religious spasm of the kind once spoken of amongst the old ones, when they did not know that we were listening in to their every word, when they mistakenly thought that we were sleeping.

One, two, three, step back now, as one, as if at the end of some staged performance. They have removed the final support, with extreme care. The light is playing now about flesh, bone, nerve, eye socket, tibia, fibula, what have you. Would it not be rash to dive into too many particularities, to over-expose ourselves to over-much ratiocination? There is no evidence of imminent collapse or of extreme fearfulness. Arms project stiffly ahead, at right angles, which is exactly as it should be. No tremors supervene when we tiptoe around and around, inspecting assiduously. No murmurations are rending the air. It has proven then to be a perfect solution. We can close the door again and congratulate ourselves on something smoothly conducted, shower gifts upon each other, return to our homes, our offices, bring the weather back, call on the traffic once again to goad and frustrate us, invite chefs, waiters to prepare, serve foodstuffs for half a millennium ahead at the very least. Man, such as he is, is now upright. He is also safely locked away just in case.

When Wednesday, as it surely must, weighed down again upon us, everyone called out in unison: why must it be a Wednesday again? Could we not for once avoid it and go directly to Thursday, which is so much closer to Friday? There was much umming and aahing about this outlandish request, but in the fulness of time it was granted, and Wednesday was delicately removed from the calendar. Yet the advocates of Wednesday, those who had invested so much in that day, having died on a Wednesday or been born on a Wednesday or fallen in love on a Wednesday or scored the goal of a lifetime on a Wednesday or sacrificed some Isaac or other on a Wednesday or baked the greatest cake of their lives on a Wednesday, all drew themselves up as one and issued an almighty protestation. No, they all bellowed, let it be *Thursday* if it is to be any day at all. Thursday, the most ugly on the tongue, is surely the one which must be sacrificed. No one loves it. Everyone loathes it. Everyone leaps over it in order to reach blessed Friday, which the entire world knows to be the best and most favoured and most beauteous day of the week. And all the while Friday sat idling on his throne, chinking his coins in his deepest pocket, scratching his fleas, and yawning and whiffling to his heart's content. In short or long, he knew himself to be wholly unassailable.

Not a single life was to be had. A few withered sticks. A fistful of dead couch grass. Two spokes of a wheel. Nothing more at all to speak of. Nothing to be found. Nothing to be favoured. Nothing to be loved. Nothing to be battened down upon. Nothing to be licked or slobbered over. Nothing to be appealed to, in all the wildness of extreme frustration, as if to a deaf man. No landscape to be overlooked. No coombe to be entered, warily. No alleyway to be unzipped. No tree to be climbed. No menu to be pondered upon. No dog to be despised. No cat to be embraced until, almost immediately, it slips away, over-loved. No word love to be spelled out, dreamily, all its four letters stretching away to eternity. No rain to be licked off the smooth bald pate. No life to be lived. No death to be suffered. No philosophers to be kicked into a sack and deposited, with all the rest, in a great heap just outside the city gate. No city on a hill at all. Not even a dog turd to be squelched.

Today, this being my revelatory day according to the calendar, I went at it as I had never attacked a well armed enemy in the past, with a concentrated fury. It is my way, of course. I never do things by half. I leap. I cry out. I suffer the consequences for days or years. That is my character, with which you are now becoming familiar as I write myself into existence for you, you who had never known me before, you who had not even guessed at the possibility that such a one as myself could even exist on this earth, because you had lived a life so idle, so rich, so somnolent, that you had never looked about you, eyes cunningly narrowed, to find me. And here I am now in front of you, hopping from foot to foot, grimacing horribly, laying out for you the best of my points of favour, seeking to justify my differences, to let you know, with accustomed vehemence, that the world need not necessarily be thus and thus and thus, it could also be *me,* and all that I am causing to percolate through its veins and arteries, with a judicious degree of slyness. I am ready to show you this world of mine now. I am ready to open it up to you, as if it were some itinerant's side-show on some street corner. You need to prepare yourself, you know. You must come at least half way to meet me. You must stir yourself from your bed, throw on a modicum of decency, step out of the door in the teeth of the wind's merciless lashing, and find me here. That is all I ask of you, and it is surprisingly little. The cost of failure – of nerve, limb, will – is almost incalculable.

Three. Why more? Many have asked for more. They have told me that the world consists of teeming millions, and all coming at you from every direction at once, to such an extent that we must collapse and weep, in a desperate heap, when we even so much as raise our eyes to see them. And it is for this reason that I have arrived at this perfectly ingenious solution. A maximum of three, one to dig, one to serve, one to receive, open-mouthed. It is all perfectly simple. I hear you then ask, blabbing off to the side in the manner of the utter irrelevance of what you are and what you have always been: what of later? Will there be a later when three will become six or even ten, when the diggers slightly exceed the open mouths, and the server has stubbed her toe on the edge of the giant copper pan and, rather than fleetly and usefully serving, is now hobbling like a crone? The fact is that all such considerations are quite beside the point. We must live forever (as it were) in the deliciously convenient and pampered nowness of three. There is nothing else worth thinking about. Calm yourself then.

The bell began to ring today. I put it away. I laid it aside. I pronounced the death rites over it, with such insolence. It would not be put away. It would not be set aside. It tolled again. And again. With such grave and slow defiance and deep-down solemnity. It outstared me. It outwitted me. It outthought me. It outfaced me. I stuffed wads of gum into my ears, and then I slept for a little while. During those thin hours of troubled sleep, the bell removed the gum from my ears with extraordinary dexterity, and then lodged itself in my inner ear in order that its presence should be that much more emphatic and undeniable. I became the bell then, at the summit of the bell tower, helplessly, furiously swinging. All day and all night I swung from side to side, ever more violently. My entire skull became the bell, lurching and banging around so dizzily. My brain became the bell. I had no other thoughts but tolling and tolling. I understood the importance of the bell as I had never known it before, I knew its centrality in our lives, how it called out to us, always, and with such urgency, to prayer, to new life, to death, to fasting, how it caused us to run hither and thither like mad things on fire, seeking out the most profound meanings of its incessant tollings. I felt grateful that I had become the bell, and that the bell had become me, to the depths of my innermost being, this bell that I had failed to understand for so long. My answer to your question? Yes, my name is John Bell.

There is no advantage to be gained from uneven ground. The point is to be fleet of foot and utterly dependable, to arrive at one's destination at the appointed hour, the appointed minute, just in time to see the man with the stop watch preparing to yank it out of his fob pocket and point down at its dial even as he frowns – and not a second later. Uneven ground impedes human movement, human progress. A toe is stubbed. Unaccustomed weariness interposes itself. Unanticipated obstacles present themselves in the form of stones, fissures, gaping holes in the ground into which a small man or two might all too easily fall. My worst example of this came only yesterday, when I found two short, svelte old men lodged in the same narrow fissure, two former friends who had been there for upwards of seven years, and who were now able to survive – only just – on the hunks of moistened bread that were being carelessly tossed down to them from time to time by innumerable exasperated passers by. Every man who looked down as he hurried on by made the same comment: there is really no advantage at all to uneven ground if such impediments as this hove into view, slowing every necessary journey to a snail's pace. Hill climbers, hearing of this, rose up as one in fury.

My task is first to step aside, quite deftly, and then to measure the bricks with an extraordinary degree of accuracy when they have fallen. It is not my job to watch them falling, to comment on their general direction of flight, or to have any opinion whatsoever on such subjects as the desirability of armed conflict between near neighbours, general warfare, machines of war, demolition, or wanton destruction. None of that is within my remit. All that will be taken care of in due course by men better equipped than myself to deal with such matters. My task is merely to measure each brick – length, breadth, depth - and to prepare a list of bricks and their various sizes for those who will need to consult it by and by. I have even been told that this list of mine will prove to be very useful in times to come because there will be those who will appear in our midst with the express intent of building again, of laying one brick upon another and then another, of shaping entire rising walls of brick at right angles to each other at the corners of new buildings, and finally of causing many human beings to enter in, even ushering them indoors with scatterings of delightful words such as comfort, home and security, all of which have been expunged from our vocabulary.

I asked you only to knock. You have no other purpose. The world made you for this. It knew what it was up to. Knocking is a primal act, be it on skull or door. Rap. Rap. Rap. What happens then? If on skull, you find yourself alert to some form of enquiry from beyond the self. Something is happening outside the doors of the skull of which you are not yet fully aware. You gather together your bones. You clothe them with flesh. You prepare the rictus grin for the world. And then you ask the question: why in the world's name were you knocking when I have nothing to say to you? Why need you enquire of me when I gave my last answer years ago, and there is simply no more to be said? You listen out for the answer. There is no answer. What you said was unanswerable, you know that well enough. And the consequence? That knocking again. And so it goes on. There will only ever be knocking from now on. And you will be doing the knocking – you, yes you – because you deserve no better, do you?

The merest chink of light. Prise it open, to left and to right, pull at it, heaving. There! That is a little better. It falls full on your left shoe now. See how that toe cap blazes! That is proof enough, is it not? Then the light begins to shrink again, to draw in, diminish, and you begin to sweat. You have seldom known such exasperation – that the light should begin to diminish again after it had appeared to be opening out at your behest! Opening out like a peacock's fan! What is happening then these days? You tiptoe across to the cupboard and open the door. How many times have you opened this door? Why answer such a question when it exists only to taunt you? You take out each one, each lidded jar, one by one. Twenty-seven on the front row alone. Reassuring enough. No need to scrabble around at the back then, gathering dust on the sleeve. You know that there are ranks and ranks of them, ranged in their rows, and all prepared to step forward to do their duty. That is the way of a lidded jar, to do its duty, uncomplaining. And so just the one will do. You unscrew the lid. You remove it. You stare down and into the little pot of light, seeing how it has curdled there. It glows up at you so warmly. You go to dip your finger in. You are wholly reassured. It is as if your entire body is invested with human warmth, as if you have learnt once again how to talk.

Come back here and look, I say to her, raising my voice for the first time in hours. Was I sleeping just then? Is this why the recent past has been so unclear to me, why I seemed to be drifting like a small boat pushed along by the merest puff of a breeze? I don't know. How could I know? Don't even ask me. See to the condition of your own moth-eaten sleeve. Look now, there... Look! I say it again. My appeal has become a little more peremptory. Are you coming? Are you listening? These are the words I am thinking. It is morning again outside this window, and the children, those sun-drenched, happy children, are playing in the shrubbery as they always do, with their sticks and their balls, pushing them along again with the love and the patience and the sheer, no-holds-barred determination that only children seem able to muster. I wish I had such patience. I wish I was a child again, pushing that ball ahead of me. Are you still a child then? What height are you now when you approach me in response to my question, when you come sidling up beside me? Of differing heights, I would say, depending upon how quickly I look away, and then look back at you in order to refresh my looking. You open your mouth, and once again you say these words which are just beyond my hearing. Why must this always be happening, that your words are just beyond my hearing? You even smile at me and point down at the children. No, at one child in particular, the one who is looking up at you, the one who is crying and who is now being restrained, quite forcefully. It wishes to rush to the door. You are calling back to it, and still I do not hear you. I have an urge to rush towards the door myself in order that I might play my part in this urgent life's game, but my part once again is unclear to me, and now you are frowning up at me, as you always frowned up at me, and I am so much regretting that I said those words to you: come back here and look. Look. Look!

In the corridor. Queuing in the corridor. Once again. Nine or ten of us. Or perhaps more. Light just a little too low to tell at this late-afternoon hour... All showing the patience of lambs ha ha. Some leaning, fierce elbow-jutting against walls, or bending over as if to stretch, loudly yawning, arms swinging to the accompaniment of deep sighs, or bolt upright, bullet-headed, with crossed arms and eyes blazing, boots well spread, as though ready for anything. Will there be anything? Has there been anything yet? Not yet. And also watches, looking down regularly at watches, as if by staring down at a watch with a look of fury and impatience might somehow speed up the process of queuing, as if the door into which we must finally enter is full of those counterparts of ours, who will be staring down at watches too, sharing a genuine belief that watches are of great importance, that we must abide by and take heed of the lessons of watches, that we must look out for the moment – surely it will come, that moment? – when watches finally lose their patience, and we all burst into the room together and shout out in chorus: Why so long?

Why have you kept us all here for so long? Who are we to be made to live like this? And all spoken into a room with windows open to chilling air and grey skies, with chairs unoccupied. Many chairs. Perhaps twenty or thirty or more. At least that if not more. And all set at very perplexing angles, as if in preparation for huddles of heated conversation concerning matters of defence, accusation and denunciation.

The rage rose to the height of the throat, and then, little by little, it receded again, falling finally to the level of the ankle, where it remained until approximately seven o'clock, at which hour it disappeared altogether because at that hour the drinking began, the furious drinking, in which all sorrow and all rage drowned until approximately two o' clock of a winter's morning, when he sat bolt upright in his bed, and the rage was back much as before, in full fury, to such an extent that he would stuff his mouth with a pillow to prevent a bellowing out so loud and so furiously insistent that all the neighbours would come running and beat on the door in fury.

I could not have asked for more than what you gave me. It was always more than enough, just as you yourself were always more than enough when I had you, and now that I do not have you, you feel to me even more than that in all your fierce, sputtery, posthumous blazing. You weigh upon me now in all your splendour, in all your insistent lightning-boltery. But in those days of yore and yon, how you would come upon me, and then not let go of me for weeks together, waking or sleeping! To such an extent in fact that from time to time I would need to slip out of myself as a small man might slip out of a sloppy, over-large suit with padded shoulders, and tiptoe away into the shrubbery nearby in order to drink and to smoke and to complain of how this maddening, here-and-gone world wildly topsy-turvys – in fact to do what others generally do, the normal things of life, which had, it seems, almost always been passing me by because your presence had always been so insistently overwhelming. And now that I no longer have you close by and here with me, I can praise and appraise all that you were. I can pick out each small particle of you and hold it up to the light as if it were a small pearl or a piece of grit in the sock or the shoe and ask myself over and over: was it really thus then with her? Can I really believe all this to have been true, I mean truly true?

Yes, I do agree, it was an accident, how all this happened, the way this road, this very particular road, shaped itself, and the hills rose up beside the road, one on each side, channelling the cars into a narrow and umbrageous groove between, those cars which would be moving, always moving, in two very particular directions. I woke up and I found it so, accidentally present to me. And when I describe how it is to others, they disagree with me, and they invite me to stand beside the road and to see for myself. But the road to which they always introduce me is not this road at all, in spite of the fact that it seems to occupy the very same terrain outside my mean and narrow bathroom window. It is distinctively different, and I behave towards it, when I see it, not at all as I behave when I confront the miraculous accident of my own road. I close my eyes in order to expunge their road from my vision – the sight of it out there maddens me so – and I tell them, with modesty and patience and good will and all the accuracy that I can muster, just how much the road I remember differs from theirs. They tell me that I grow angry when I speak, and that it is for this reason that several men must arrive to restrain me and wrestle me inside the back of a vehicle. I recognise no such anger. I recognise, yes, a characteristic vehemence and an extreme intolerance of lies, but I would go no further than that. So much pivots, always, about the nature of what is to be regarded as the truly accidental. Those are my parting words to them, spoken as if from some podium, before they carefully place the gag over my mouth.

It was one of those incremental days again, when nothing comes on too quickly, and everything amounts to nothing more than a small peeking out from behind door, window, chair, what have you. I like such days. I suck on them as a child might just suck on a boiled sweet, for its brief *hallelujah gadzooks* acclaim in the mouth! That was it then, all that it amounted to, not much it has to be said, shifting from chair to chair or from sipped cup to ankle, scratching the same, with fury, when it itched, which it did, often, and also seeing her there a little out of the corner of my eye, ignoring me altogether, spending another of those long and sanctimonious days of hers in which she regards me as an irrelevance for all my foolish ways. And I tell her again, just the once, though less and less these days because she mocks me so, I am a philosopher, I say it, dead-pan, pulling the old cracked and despised orange bic pen from the left trouser pocket, and driving it up in the direction of my nostrils in order to prove that I am in fact nothing but a holy fool of the kind that she has chosen to despise, being so deep down atheistical on account of some sad old priest's roving fingers.

Memory plays with me as a child plays with a toy. See this, it says, and shows me: a lawn rolling out with a big blue pram coming on, or a seaside scene with the squeal of a gull, or a child weeping over a broken nothing at all. But when I go to walk a little closer, casually strolling over, and seeming not to care overmuch as is my way, the whole thing withdraws from me in an almighty rush, and I hear his mockery again behind the hedge, and I kick out for want of better. There is nothing there when I go to look. There is always nothing there. And so I clam up, and I affect a certain engaging sullenness. Now would you not call that delightful if you were to choose one adjective amongst the teeming many?

Well, why not, given that it has happened again, and the two of us must have conspired to make it happen? Yes, why not? I have turned up in a suits of sorts, the tried and threadbare one, and you have your heels on, the old heels, higher than most, vintage you call them. We putter along together, being dazzled by lights a little too bright for us.

You point out this and that – fluffballs, nothing more – in some high-piled, Christmas-frenzied window, which I look at, momentarily. It is dark now, the mood of which pushes us a little closer, hip against hip, swaying a little as we walk, almost moving towards a dance step or two, but not quite, never quite dancing. We stop for a jar or two in the old place, low-beamed, low-ceilinged. I watch the fizz skimming the surface of your glass, and how those bubbles, when neatly transferred, seem to speak of the quality of your lips, which are also a little fuller than usual. I sigh to myself as I inwardly survey such unspoken terrain. Meanwhile, the big, narrow-eyed men with their finicky finger ends throw darts at the board high on the wall in the corner, on and on, biting their lips. From time to time I hit on something to say to you, seldom much, but perhaps just enough, at which you often smile a little coyly, face bowed to the glass. I speak of bus timetables, drenchings by rain on the walk to the garage, my mother's habit of over-cooking the vegetables. You take it all in. You make of it what you will. Something tremendous is racing somewhere beyond the door. Some man evidently has his foot down.

The Waiting Room. It says so on the door. It had said so in the corridor, with that arrow – black and decisive – pointing to the door, which is somewhat ajar. We all move in, shuffling, shuffling, having queued with such patience. Since dawn, could it have been? Since the dawn before last, we all agree, nodding affirmatively, and also gnashing our teeth. Then we are all in there together. So little space for so many. The chairs are all occupied, the hard wooden benches, the shelves, even the narrowest shelves, up there high on the wall, are occupied by legs wantonly dangling, a child's legs kicking out, until they are stilled by the firm slap of a hand. All waiting. All patiently waiting. I look up at the sign again over the door, steadily lit as it surely has always been. Nothing else. Nothing more. Who needs more? There is only the one door. Why need another door? What would be its purpose? To where would it lead? We need nowhere else. We know full well why we are all here, in silence. In order to wait. And then to wait for a little bit more. No one guesses at the hour.

There is no hour. The light above the door is steady, and it remains so for the duration. Some smaller ones are seated on the floor, against the walls, legs tight drawn up, forehead on knees. Inward contemplation, that is what it must be. What else but that? You say to me: what are we all waiting for? I shrug my shoulders at the sheer absurdity of the question. There is no *purpose* in waiting. There is only the waiting. That *is* the purpose of waiting. That is why we sit here, in this Waiting Room. That is why no further words are necessary. It is all so clean, so simple, so everlasting.

And then she took the stairs, those steeply climbing stairs, two by two, ahead of me, with all the vitality of youth fresh sprung and singing. And then a whistle blew, and two quick young men removed the stairs, dismantling them – treads, risers, edges – so quickly that I had to laugh to myself at the celerity of it all. What next then? She moved across the room ahead of me. I simply could not keep pace with her, no matter how hard I tried. She was so sylvan-swift and so beautifully, bountifully tall and lissome, just as I would have wished. And I had so wished before I first saw her, which caused her to smile at me, beneficently, as I noticed when she tossed back her head, momentarily. How did she know that though, what was hidden in my thoughts? And then they lifted the room away, seconds after we had left it – I had to skip aside in order to avoid their almightily eager onrush. Lifted it directly up into the air, and then tossed it from hand to hand as if it were a game of many, many players. Such men these were! And what a woman this was! What next then? Her voice streamed ahead of me, down a corridor, dark and ever darker. And then I stumbled. I stumbled and fell. The men came on and picked me up and tossed me into her arms, high up I went, and then down, down into her arms, never had there been a fall quite so smooth and so even. And yet she was not looking at me as she caught me. How then *did* she catch me? And yet she had caught me! By some miracle she *had* caught me. You too called it a miracle when I told you, at the bus stop, later, as we laughed fit to burst asunder, like some child's red balloon popping. Such things do happen!

I am not a ghost. Nor are you. Both of us are flesh, blood, bone and what have you. Tap on this skull of mine. Harder if you like! See how I wince when I do it, see what anger I show. No wonder. Flesh, blood, bone are inclined to anger when you harm them. It is a form of fight-back. Who would willingly have his head stove in with a hammer? With a ghost, it is quite other. A ghost flits in and out, willy-nilly, feather-light, never quite stopping, without a thought in its head, because it has no head to speak of, no head, that is, of flesh, blood, bone (and what have you). No ghost sits in a chair. No ghost *depresses* a chair. No ghost mopes and eats sausages all evening, quite slowly, and then leaves the plate, all smeary with ghost-licks, in the sink. That is not their way. They are too fanciful, too flighty. A ghost eats nothing but empty air. That is more than sufficient, to chew on empty air as if it were food that gave satisfaction. Yes, a ghost is an absurdity. Which is why I have no truck with them. What is more, none of my bygone friends is inclined to contradict me.

<hr>

Guess what happens next. You raise two fingers into the passing traffic. The next thing you know, you are in bed with a smeary grey sky outside the window, which looks hard into you, you, a disagreeable man of forty or so with a raging temperature, and no one to bother at all because your behaviour is intolerable, life-long. No one to have and to hold you. You scarcely wish to prop yourself up at a bar if the truth be known. Get rid of it all then. Wind back to the beginning. A drooling babe in a cradle, legs kicking out. Then the rain falls in buckets, and you are a boy foot-slogging uphill to school, where you sulk and you scheme and you make nothing of yourself. Your mother aids and abets you, and you steal money from her purse, and jack-the-lad around the neighbourhood until she dies all of a sudden, clipped by a bike stepping out at a turn, and leaves you nothing (but a little something). Having nothing, you *are* nothing. You sell the house and rent a room in a house very similar. You learn the virtues of sitting and idling until someone similar befriends you, making a smoking (smoking and tippling) party – for two in a room with a sofa, from whom you steal a little each week until he notices, and out you go again. Guess what happens next, guess whose life you are inclined to vomit forth.

The noises off are not your noises. Nor do they belong to her. Is she more than anything but a distant memory? The rushing past this door has nothing to do with you either. Best would be to attach the board to the window frame – an exact fit! – and to paint in the scene of the moment. So there you go. All done. Your legs, streetwise and a little dandified, carry you by again, as they always would. You pay attention to so little. You pay attention only to your legs and how they move. No one speaks to you until your prepare the words they are to say. You are busy at that all day, scripting what others are to say to you, how their words make a carefully measured and delineated curve around the outer limits of your own, as if paying homage in some strange way. You are Saturn and their words are the moons of Saturn, turning as you turn, never approaching, always in attendance, settled, and utterly removed out there, contented too, in their appointed places. Is not all that engaging? Then you remove the board, and wipe it all off again. You say nothing all the rest of the day. All that conjuring has quite exhausted you. You stow the board in the attic. You take off your head, your arms. You make an incision and remove your heart, perfectly painlessly, and stow that too. Then you shut the door and turn your back on it all. Peace. Perfect peace.

Charlotte took the box with the photographs from the shelf, which jutted out from the wall like her own upper teeth pushed out her upper lip. She was not, certainly not, a great beauty. That box seemed so heavy today. She could barely lift it. And yet inside there were the same seven photographs, curling up at the edges, tinged that pale egg-yellow, which had changed either as much or as little as she herself had changed. As ever, it was Aunt Emeralda who took her in hand first. Well no, not exactly, because it was she who had Aunt Esmeralda in hand, holding her steady at waist height, cradling her on her knees, which bounced a little as she stared, a little anxiously. She was standing beside the wash tub, holding her huge bundle of laundry out to the side. What arms she had, that woman, and what a fierceness of regard! It was always Aunt Esmeralda who took her aside and button-holed her in this way. Why then did she always choose *her* when there were various mild-mannered others she might have chosen, small cousins, thin of arm, stick-legged, who did nothing but kick balls or throw a stick to a silly spotted dog who never failed to be poised mid-air in its eager leap to catch? Yes, it was always Aunt Esmeralda, her grandmother's second cousin and not an aunt at all, who would not let her go, who always knew how little she had done, what man she had not met, the fact that she had failed to discharge even the most meagre portion of her chores again. It was more than enough to stare at her to know all this, to know it for sure, just as surely as God lived inside his church, that it was this and only this that Aunt Esmeralda was thinking about her, because her mouth was pulled down at the left side and, generally speaking, she had that terrible look of chastisement radiating from her very stout and rigid person. And so she found herself saying it all over again, what she always said, every time she took the photograph out, blurting it out before Aunt Esmeralda even spoke, and without even wishing to do so because it caused her so much pain to speak in this way: Aunt Esmeralda (and, yes, she knew she was not an aunt, not really), I know that I have done wrong, and that I need to do better, and that I have not grown up in any way at all since we last spoke...When she put the box away later, having carefully wiped away all the tears from her eyes, she found herself asking out loud: Could that really have been only yesterday that we spoke?

If I could mutter one prayer to God above in the fulness of my anger, it would be this one. You are an evil thing with your staring, yellow eyes and your venomous discharge, and I hate you more than I hate even the most deadly of poisonous snakes because you prey upon this world worse than any lion or tiger or cobra has ever preyed upon other helpless beasts. If I could say one prayer to God, it would be this one, but I cannot pray it. My mouth is locked against it. I know that I cannot say these words because I am too afraid of what might happen to myself and others were I to do so. I have had such a gentle and tender family encircling me all the days of my life, from the moment I first blinked awake and felt their presence about me. They are so tender and so watchful. They are also elderly now and extremely fragile, and I would fear for their safety if a vengeful God came marauding through these parts, seeking me out. And yet I know now – it has only just occurred to me as I wrote these words – that I have a great deal to fear. The fact is that I have told you of this unspoken prayer, just now, that I have blurted it out recklessly, and does not God know our innermost thoughts? Does he not know already, thanks to the mere fact that I have shared the words of my unspoken prayer with you, exactly how much I hate him? In which case, we are all utterly helpless, and we must prepare ourselves for his vengeance...

I could have asked her. I know I could have asked her. And yet I did not ask her. I asked myself instead. And yet the questions I asked myself were not the questions I would have asked her. They were different questions. In fact, they were quite beside the point, and I knew that even as I heard myself muttering them over to myself. I knew how much of a smokescreen I was throwing up, and how irrelevant these words were to me, and, what is more, that they prevented me asking the questions that I really wanted and needed to ask. What species of helplessness held me back? More to the point though, surely, is now to ask this: Why did I not ask her myself? Why had I resigned myself to asking the questions of myself when I knew that all I had to do was to set down the glass, rise up from this chair, leave this studio apartment on the nineteenth floor, and, having padded feline-quietly across the threadbare-carpeted floor, gently knock on her door? Then I might have heard her come walking, a little gingerly, no doubt, towards her door, and ask in that thin, reedy, troubled voice of hers who exactly had arrived to disturb her on a day when she, above all things else, wished not to be disturbed, when she wished to be alone with herself and her cat and her radio stations, flipping hurriedly from one to another as if there were meaning to be found somewhere, in some random voice coming over from somewhere or nowhere, perhaps even in a language that she did not quite understand. Not my voice though, oh no. Never my voice. Some other's sufficiently unlike mine to please her. Yes, there was still so much for me to forget about her. And, needless to say, for her still to forget about me.

When you switch on a light in any room – this one, say – it is as if the voice of conscience is speaking back at you with the utmost urgency. The difficulty is, always, that you never quite know what exactly it is that conscience wishes to say to you other than to reprimand you for being who you are. When that happens, I stare down at my hands. I examine them, turning them back and forth as one might flip a small flounder in a pan. They are clean and utterly docile, these hands of mine, with well pared nails. They are not hands to whom woman or man would ever be inclined to take exception. Why then are they always so restless, these hands? Why do they always itch – morning, noon, night – to turn on the light in order that the questioning, the endless and tedious questioning, might begin again? Why would these hands, these useful and harmless and faithful and innocent hands, want that to happen? They have been good for so many things in their time, these hands: the careful opening of doors onto the freshness of new worlds, for example. They are almost my eyes, these hands of mine. Why then would they wish to provoke me into endeavouring to answer innumerable questions to which there can never be any answers?

She was always such a solace to me. That's how I always thought of her: as a solace. As a duck board is a solace when thrown across a shallow stream. As steaming hot tea in a mug, firmly embraced between two hands, is a solace after a long, cold, hard journey. I would never wish it to be otherwise. I would even call her by that name: Solace. *Sister Solace.* She had no other. The name filled her to the very top and overbrimming. On days when the rain drove so hard that it leaped – like a champion hurdler – over the stoup and poured into the room, setting even my bed afloat, she would rise up in front of me in her wimple, with her soothing words, and her rising and falling, arm-and-hand gestures of slow command. And then, little by little, as the rain subsided, shrinking back to the sea, which seemed a little cowed, if not humbled, by her presence near me as I wrung out my pants, a certain calmness would return to me. Best of all was to be led by the hand down to the jetty in order to contemplate together the water's unfathomable mysteries. At a certain moment of beatific calm between us, she would toss her wimple onto the waters, and together we would watch it float and float, or bob and float and lean, until it was entirely lost to view. In short: Sister Solace tamed me.

There could never be a better moment than this to give praise for humanity. No audience could be quite so well prepared as we are. In the fish market over there, they have all downed tools – saws, hammers, gutting knives of all shapes and sizes, from the murderously brutal to the surprisingly small and finicky – and now they are streaming towards us, two by two, up the long, slippery jetty. Even the abiding stench of fish on their aprons will not be too much for us. Soon they will all be at the door. Soon they will be joining us. As will the prisoners from jails strewn everywhere, with such lawless abandon, about this lawless country. The great double doors will all open up, and thousands of slick-haired, mild-mannered, furtive men, the ripest crop of criminality ever put on public view, will all come here too to stand with us in solidarity. Yes, they too will be ready. By the time that he rises to speak, there will be many more than we harried two or three to applaud our achievements. As the Bible is true, so too are these words of mine true, driven hard down like nails into a board. There is much to be said for humanity. For our common humanity, that is.

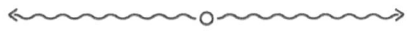

Caught in the act of being oneself! Unavoidable, they always say, no matter how many doors to be hiding behind, and there are always so many of those. Caught in the act of being unwilling to crawl or to rise from beneath the sheets in order to avoid the need to enter into the fulness (or the half-fulness) of the being that one may have chosen to become. Who was it then? Who exactly is he to be? There is always so much dilly-dallying or shilly-shallying with this and that – trousers here or a wisp of a shirt there. The thrust of a dwindling, tubular arm, or the flapping forth of a dangling leg. All so ridiculous! And all so makeshift too! And then, having once become, to doubt whether it is really true at all because so much seems to be going so tragically amiss with that day's coy – or perhaps not so coy! – self-presentation. Voice too blaring-full, or so empty of content that it barely issues in the meekest of mouse squeaks when all's said and done. What *is* to be done then? There is nothing to be done except in this very daily doing, on and on. Unless, of course, the mood of resignation brings about or issues in – with all the raw inevitability of any old stream train squeezing in to any old station, with a clank and a roar and a rude belching of smoke fit to destroy any human lung – the ogling of stacked boxes, long and solemn and makeshift things of such poor workmanship that no half decent man would ever wish to be caught dead in one.

April always comes back to me as if it had never been away. The scents of April. The gentle showers of April. The hyacinths of April. And especially when it is *not* April. It was in April that I first caught at your arm beside the road, when you were about to step forth dangerously into the traffic. No! I said, and yanked you back. You were a child just then, and I a man, doing my daily walk, back and forth, looking out for the good of the neighbourhood as I put it to myself, I, with my settled saintly halo, a little dull, a little earnest. You cried when I yanked your arm, and then you understood why I had done it, and you thanked me. Years later, standing beside a trestle table, I offered you juice in a glass. When you inclined your head up to mine to accept it, I recognised that same look in your eye, that child's fearful look. You did not remember me. I am not a memorable man, it has to be said, and many may have said it. Your husband set it aside at once, quite brusquely, and gave you water, saying: thank you, but she drinks only water on public occasions such as this one. I retired then, into a corner, to think back to that April, and of how I had saved her from certain destruction. It was the finest moment of my life, I believe, and I had told no one. She had stepped back, the car had sped by, and life had continued, in all its hazards and all its blandnesses. But to me it was my finest moment, to have done that thing, and as I reached for my brown overcoat again within half an hour – it could have been no more than that – of having arrived at the church hall, I stepped forth into the sunshine of a late December morning with a certain pride, a pride seldom experienced heretofore.

There are many more words than you could ever wish to use! I taunt you with those words. I bellow them out into the air within your hearing in order to humiliate you. That is why you avoid me, because I burden you with so many words, heaping them upon your head, or flinging them after you as you hurry away from me, fine, well-turned, latinate, polysyllabic, Miltonic words of the kind faithfully and carefully stowed away only in dictionaries. That is where I live my rich and fulfilling life, within the pages of many dictionaries, with my torch and my eyeglass, digging ever deeper into dictionaries, preferably the old ones. I spend whole days together down there, a deep-cast miner of words. Clothes mean nothing to me. Abluting this body means nothing to me – let it stink to high heaven! I have no time for such irrelevancies. There is too much steady accumulation to be done, and each day offers me twenty-four hours only in which to do it. What am I to do with these words now that you have refused to listen to me, now that you have left me here to my own devices? The question is an irrelevance. I do not need to justify this pursuit. When they are all present in front of – and behind and beside – me, I need do nothing but admire their magnificence as they stretch away and away from me. These words speak for themselves.

The horse came to enquire of us what had happened to its rider. So far it had been an unexceptionable day in the life of a horse. A man unknown to it had stepped briskly enough into the stable, whistling shrilly through his teeth, and had confidently flung his leg over. The horse had looked out for Mr Denham just then, the stable hand who was, by and large, responsible for handing over the reins to some other, whilst simultaneously and surreptitiously introducing a cube of sugar to the horse's muzzle on the palm of his hand... None of that had happened this morning. Instead, a tall man, making a single agile leap, had flung his leg over, seized hold of the reins, taken control, and off they had gone, for miles and miles, at quite a brisk pace. All morning he had sung at the top of his voice as if all of life were nothing but a bright-shining opportunity, urging the horse on, on at a pace uncustomarily speedy. And then, having arrived at a small, green house in the midst of nowhere, he had slipped out of the saddle and arrived at the door at a brisk run, which had then opened for him as if it had been waiting... The horse patiently watched the sun taking its customary course up, over and down the sky, and when night came on, knowing not what to do, had wandered off to seek assistance elsewhere. Needless to say, we took it in, and now it sleeps with our house boy in the garage. Each is pleased with this arrangement. For good or ill – I let you choose – we had been unable to answer its questions.

Most of the day there is no one here. No one, that is, apart from the usual inhabitants, who push shapeless lumps of stinking food back and forth across enamel plates, a noise I find completely intolerable most days. That is why I choose to describe them all as No One because the someone – or perhaps even the some*ones* – that I am still to choose has not yet presented himself at my bedroom door, although from time to time I do believe that I begin to hear a small and increasingly eager clamour out there, at which point I rise up on my elbow and cry out: is he here? And then the harsh one with the close-cropped hair – she is usually brandishing a vile looking broom – pokes her head around the door and says, baldly: no, stay asleep until you are spoken to. And then I fall asleep again. I have made clothes for this man who is to come out of my very own bed sheets, would you believe as much. I would. I would. I lie back here, hour after dreamy hour, stroking them with my own hands. There is a grey frock coat, and a pair of tightish tan breeches to enhance his bumps and his glides and his folds. There are even some shoes, black as the flash of his gleaming eye! I found an old iron last in the cellar, some shoe leather, nails, hammer, what have you, and I made them myself. They are so magnificent. And I know that they will fit him perfectly because it was whispered to me by someone, early one morning, the exact size that would be required. They nestle just beneath the side of the bed, out of the way of her broom, or she could so easily take a swipe at them and set them spinning under, which would render them irretrievable because I find it so difficult to move. But when he arrives, I know that my strength will be restored. I shall clothe him head to toe, and we shall dance together, out of the door, down the corridor, and gone forever. Adieu one and all! And adieu to all stinking foodstuffs, too!

Mathematics is a game for a single player. I climb this infinite series of prime numbers with the courage of a man who is shinning, two rungs at a time, up the dull of an aluminium ladder to heaven. I can even see the stars from here, and observe how they wheel around me, dizzyingly. Even the small ones, the ones, the twos and the threes, are so playful, and so modest into the bargain. They make no claims for themselves. They pretend to be nothing other than careful and steady accumulations of each other, all heaping up so patiently hour by hour. And yet there is no stopping them. They start so small. They grow so large. I am in such a state of ceaseless admiration. And then there are the games that we play, the subtraction games, for example. You think you have someone here, and then, in a second, with the side swipe of the hand, he is gone, absent, no longer in being at all. I do not know whether they live or they die. They do not tell me. They live for me, for sure. Would *you* tell me? Do you know?

This landscape, so widely outspreading, was the latest bargain. She came to me with it on a tray, nestled in beside the safety matches. I know a bargain when I see one, and so I seized it immediately, not caring at all that I had scattered the safety matches, all six boxes of them, across the road. I find so little time to complain these days, with all this landscape of mine to see to. It is so time-consuming. The least of it − you simply could not have guessed at this − is the range of hills which rise and rise where plain gradually gives way to deciduous forest. In fact, just beyond that. Would you walk there in all your infirmity? I do. But I am still much younger than you are, and in the grip of this towering ambition, which has been a life-long affliction. And so I took the lake-side walk, the one that leaves you pretty well in shadow until tea time, and there I paused, not really being able to believe my luck. Sure there had been good days before, several of them at a run, but nothing quite like this. If things go on in this way, several single-storey bank buildings may yet spring up at my feet, with tellers slowly coming at me on their knees offering me fat rolls of greenbacks. Would I need it? I leave you to answer a question quite as silly as that one. I am a man with needs after all, and there is no telling when the winds will sweep down from the hills − as the Assyrians once did, mind − and upend me once again as if I were a dolt.

To own a pair of nutcrackers is to be in the shadow of something quite formidable, a something which keeps you awake at nights unless you have had the good sense − not me − to stow a bottle of essence of lavender in the shallow drawer of the corner table. I hold them in my hand regularly, dandling them − the feel of them there gives me such cheap pleasure − but all that happens by and by is that a character from a rather poor novel comes along − some sad-sack cynic needless to say − and asks me, rather glibly: where are the nuts, my friends? Or: what's with the flat-trousered look these days, pal? No pal of mine. Even when this happens − and it is often − it does not stop me because to be the owner of such a pair of nutcrackers as these raises me to such a height in my own estimation that I feel capable of looking down on anyone who spits in my face, which happens quite often. And when it does, I simply wipe it off. It is as easy as that – and then I go on. Week after week I go on – you could watch me if you took the bus here – seeking out that which I need in order to get, finally, into action: brazil nuts, walnuts, hazel nuts, and all tricked out in their hard shells, ripe for the cracking. That is my dream, and I guess that it is the dream of many, is it not? Is not every word of this true, by your own dim lights?

I had this dream of water once, that it dripped down into my mouth while I was sleeping. But no part of that dream was true. When I opened my eyes, the land was as badly cracked as ever (those cracks resembled fissures of lightning), and, as usual, not a soul was stirring from the ground. There we all still lay, foetally locked into each other, because we were just too parched to stir. Can you imagine how dry lips must become when no water exists to moisten them, and what pain we must all suffer when we try to move them? It is like trying to heave open an ancient, jammed door. That is our current situation exactly, and it has been like that since at least a week last thursday, though I cannot really believe that it does not stretch back much further than that. Would you spare us some water if you had a little more than you needed? Are you likely to answer my letter of request if I were to write it? Needless to say, I will not be writing such a letter because I am too weak to heave myself up onto my left elbow, too weak to then crawl over to grandmother's old, fold-down teak desk to look for writing paper, and too weak to apply a stamp to the envelope even were I to find one, because, needless to say, I would have no spittle to moisten such a stamp. So you could say – and I am saying it for you – that all this, quite conveniently, lets you off the hook.

Friendship is this glue which binds us, the tall with the short, the tractor with the combine harvester in the field, all this is friendship which bonds us together. Speech is not necessary. Physical proximity may help a little if one protects another from the fierce driving rain by leaning over, with perhaps both arms enfolding if winds also come wheedling and knifing. Such gestures as these speak of friendship. But sometimes no gestures are necessary at all. The merest glance could suffice, across some filthy, rain-sluiced street, when so much may seem so hopeless. It may be then that the glance comes, just the one, and you accept it without demur or hesitation, you take it in for later, to ponder upon, giving thanks for its presence there just a little while ago because it had offered you more than a smidgen of hope. Not all need this kind of thing, of course. There are those who stand solemn and upright, who walk straight ahead without once glancing to left or to right, who possess such fierce and sure knowledge of their destination that no distraction is necessary at all, least of all of a sentimental kind. Such persons are buried with arms fast rigid at their sides, and no tears are wept over them because there are none to see. In this case, a ghost may be hired to fling the clods over. Ghosts spare no expense. Ghosts even care so little.

Whose Woman was the name she went by. No one claimed her. She had arrived here without warning, with a bundle at her back and a letter of recommendation, illegible too, because water had done its worst when she was sleeping beside the road. We took pity on her. We kept her with us. We spoke to her in the few words that she knew, which were not many. We tried to teach her more, and even to write them down, but she turned her head stiffly to one side when we asked her to look down, and to repeat them after us. She was faithful to us though, rather as a dog is faithful to its master, who does nothing but look and walk ahead. She grew accustomed to these parts as a dog is accustomed to sniffing the ground before turning and turning, and then lying down and sleeping where it has turned. She followed us from here to there when we did our chores, as if wishing to learn how we lived our lives, as if to emulate us. She was always alongside us or behind us or in front of us, as if blocking the way, when tears started without warning and for no particular reason. We could fathom no reason because she would not speak to us. She was never inside us. We could never quite find her here, although we did look for her. And we still look for her.

I regret a little – not a lot – that I am not the example you expected me to be. It takes much to confess this, I know. I so much wanted to measure up, to walk in with such confidence, bearing the mahogany tea tray in front of me heaped up with rings, foodstuffs and many exquisite Others for your delectation. It was not to be. I have remained small, woeful, and hole-in-corner, barely speaking when spoken to, barely looking up at all when you parp your fierce rubber horn at me. I know how it is to be ignored. Many have done so, and little by little I have grown accustomed to the small-scale tragedy of it all. What is to be done then, my mother, daughter, friend? Well, we could at least admire this road together by remarking upon how Roman it is in its arrow-straightness. Would that do? Or something else perhaps? I have brought one or two tools and my grandfather's pinking shears along. I could hurry over again with further suggestions once I have finished with this muted welcoming in of the new dawn. Believe that much of me if you will.

Sweet Solomon just keeps on walking. He knows to do nothing else. It is the entirety of his nature. Straight out of the womb, and having been set upright on the floor, and then coaxed along by that kindly doctor with slippery palms, one foot moved steadily in front of another after that, almost as if he knew that he had a purpose yet to be declared. And it has never been declared, neither to Solomon nor to any of the thousand upon thousand of onlookers who have watched him pass by tirelessly day after day, without food or water, along roads so wind-buffeted and so lonely, up hills so bare and so mist-shrouded, and always without even so much as a pause for food or water. They have cheered him along, rising so early to do so. They have observed the veins pulsing in his temples. They have seen for themselves, and been truly awe-struck by, the intensity of his gaze, the tight-squeeze of his two fists so rigid at his sides. Solomon! They have all cried out, almost in unison: We are at one with you in your ceaseless endeavours! And then they have all returned to their kitchens to sip at tea, mildly bemused by it all, knowing nothing of his purpose, and certainly too timorous ever to ask.

I have known no sights the equal of this one. That is why I sit here, hour after hour, with my sandwiches and my flask of coffee. This is the vantage point known to so few. It is what I would call – and I choose my words with some care – pre-eminent. You ask why it has been gifted to me alone, why no one else seems to know even that it exists. I tell you why. Hereabouts, everything is far too ordinary. This is a place to be passed through. It barely even has a name. It raises no expectations of any kind. It is dull and level ground. And, equally, all the voices hereabouts are dull and level too. That is why I have it all to myself. It is because I alone can see it for what it is. I alone can judge of its immensity, speak at tedious length of its virtues, describe how it fans out to left and to right of me. And so the sweet fact is that I need to be nowhere but here. Why budge? Why seek out marvels elsewhere? I am utterly contented. Long may their ignorance remain absolute!

There are always so many staircases to climb, ceaselessly climb, and usually when I am at my least energetic – at day's end, for example, when I am preparing to topple sideways into my bed like a mighty felled oak from that England of yore so beloved of us all, I fervently believe. It is then that they present themselves, in a long and receding line, one after another after another, as far as the horizon line, until my eyes blur over with the weariness of it all merely to be seeing them there. The first few are easy, needless to say – the short ones with relatively shallow steps, that is. Up I go in a hop and a skip, and I feel quite proud of myself to be waving to you all from up there, often quite lazily, as if full of pride and complacency that I have proven to be at last a man such as myself. The taller and the steeper ones I have a problem with. I say such things as this to myself as I peer up, sometimes nearly cricking my neck in my efforts to see right to the mist-shrouded top. Am I the equal of this? Is this not an exercise in futility? What is the meaning of such an exercise anyway? What will it say about me if I simply refuse and walk away? I know very well the answer to the last of these questions because the usual hundreds are coralled behind the fence nearby, waiting for me to make my latest attempts, waiting to judge me with their bestial roars or their prolonged, snake-like hissings. Why do they come here every day? Why do these staircases present themselves here at all, day after day? Why do I experience, always, this weariness nigh unto death when it happens all over again, as it always surely must, given my circumstances, and my mother's truly ominous name?

The man is a terrible gadabout. You see him, always. There is no escaping him, his ceaseless energy. It makes all of us feel utterly useless, to be observing him, hour after hour, at his world-challenging tasks. There are always so many! Who has flung so many rocks, swum so many seas, or thrown back so many shots of whisky without any perceptible loss of pluck, energy or sheer, ongoing determination? This man never sleeps. We, by comparison, we poor emasculated beings, sleep more and more and more because his towering example crushes all hope in us of the moderate challenges and possibilities of bodily normality. Our muscles, our very limbs, seem to thin and to shrivel away even as we watch him, and it seems that we cannot but watch him. No other entertainment will do for us. We are obsessed by his overwhelming, nay overbearing example. That is the truth of it. It is as if we do not deserve to take up space in this world any more, as if this world is disgraced by our mere presence here. We would question him for hour after hour about our predicament were we able to slow him down and catch him and pen him inside a cage of such and such dimensions. But who would do such a thing? He alone would be capable and, frankly, what would there be in it for him to subject himself to such an ordeal?

I had promised myself that I would sweep the floor in preparation for the day of her arrival. And I was as good as my word. I swept the floor. Or, to clarify, I should perhaps say that I swept that portion of the floor immediately inside the door, because I had no intention of sweeping the whole of the kitchen floor. Who in their right mind would wish to engage with the filth of a lifetime, given the possibility that she might not even throw a single glance in my direction when she finally presented herself at my door? I knew the routine well enough. It was so tried and tested. We would all be waiting at the door, the entire street of old men, brooms in hand, in order to make crystal clear both our readiness and our enthusiasm to be standing here, albeit fleetingly, in her presence. Would the man who had done most to prepare for her presence here succeed in the end? It was such a throw of the dice. If she were not blind this year, she might well appreciate the sight of a full head of well combed, greased-back hair. But who was to say that she herself would *not* be blind? Many of we greeters were blind. She herself had often been blind. And so I did almost nothing other than to stand here, mouth firmly closed, unsmiling. One thing I had learned down the long and dreary years was this. It did you no good whatsoever to give the game away. And, as chance would have it, she failed to appear at all that year. Several of us closed our doors at sundown in a mood of smug, settled self-satisfaction.

I have no idea what ULALOOM actually means – other than to tell you that it is a woman's name. According to some, I hasten to add. No one I have met, that is. But some who were once said to have been spoken of by neighbours' friends. That intricately distant! Not good neighbours, I hasten to add, but neighbours all the same. From time to time you can hear the word flung around, when hastening by a high fence, for example. It is just as if the wind is carrying something mysterious that it barely wishes to acknowledge, let alone transport through the air: ULALOOM. Yes, does it not sound, even to an earth-bound deist such as yourself, a little ghostly? That is why, eventually, I decided to write it down on a board in white chalk.

White chalk on a blackboard of the kind we once had in the schoolroom, where that teacher with the pale white arm would do all her slow and beautiful figuring. ULALOOM. I shivered a little when I read it over to myself. It sounded a little like music, the sweet music that the young teacher with the thin pale white arm might just hum over to herself, so quietly that we boys could not possibly hear her, as she did all that intricate figuring on the board.

And so they all said WHY? And we in our turn answered them with the exact same word: WHY? It seemed so satisfying to let it out, somewhat akin to breathing when you have been holding your breath for a dare in the schoolyard. Yes, we felt so much better after we had brought ourselves to ask that ultimate question. But what next? What was the point of then sitting there and staring at each other if we had all eternity to play with? Did went not have it within us to rise up and walk across the room, back and forth, for hours at a time? Were we not capable of prolonged speechifying of a particularly impressive kind? So why then did we hesitate? Had we perhaps been emasculated by the sound of the word itself, by our saying it like that I mean, as if we truly meant it? As if we had declared ourselves once and for all? And yet if that were indeed the case, why in god's heaven had we needed to hold back for so long? Had that not too been an impediment to our progress here? Were we not, all told, a little easier inside ourselves now that the timeless, timely word had at last been uttered? Who could say where the truth lay in all of this? We glanced furtively from one to another, the fat staring at the thin, the helpless pleading with his eyes to the calm and the forthright. Who would have the pluck, the derring do to declare his hand first on this matter? And was there even a hand spare to be declared? What could possibly be the meaning of all these questions when all is said and done?

She was a baby when I first knew her, a fat, bawling, squirming, ornery thing in a super-large, heavily padded pram on giant wheels, tricked out by a local child projects' engineer so that no amount of bodily agitation would be of any use to her. Captivity was everything that she needed when so young, for all our sakes, we agreed. And yet, and within a matter of minutes or so it seemed, she had grown to a women so tall and so noisy and so demanding that I chose to walk streets which never intersected with hers for obvious reasons. How then could I have been said, by so many, and with such careless abandon, to love her so profoundly? Because it was all true what they said, I *did* love her profoundly, and so profoundly that I could not bear to be near her because I grew so feverish and out of control whenever that happened. It took so little to set me off: the announcement of her appearance as our newly elected mayor of the principality at the village fete next tuesday, for example. The sight of her very name would set me off. I would fall to my knees and begin to bibbly-babble like a helpless child in need of the solace of a pram against whose walls I would surely be inclined to beat my head until I fell senseless. The only answer was a rest cure in Barbados of all places, where the sweet, gentle pull of the strumming of old guitar strings would surely transport me elsewhere – by which I mean somewhere other than Barbados, of course, fathead.

Let me make this plain to you before you leap up from your chair and tear at my throat. There are no prayers any more. There are too few words remaining from which a prayer might even be constructed. Am I anxious about this state of affairs? Level-headed, I would say. I know the extent of my need for words. I have always settled for very few, and even those few I have under-used because I am a man who prefers silence and solitude and, yes, the thinnest skim of wordlessness. But, I hear you say, does not solitude necessarily go hand in hand with prayers, and do not prayers need many words with which to encompass the multifariousness of the deity in whose praise we are surely encouraged to utter prayers by the thousand, night and day, in words ever outstreaming from the blubbery lips of the untutored? If that is the case, I am prepared to own no deity. Let me be sufficient unto myself, in a room such as this one, quiet as any mouse dropping onto any measure of thick-piled carpet, with nothing but the sussurations of the sea just beyond the window to idly attend to, which, needless to say, I do not hear in any truly convincing way, because the window always remains fast closed against every conceivable variety of menace on a Tuesday such as today is rapidly becoming.

This is where it all begins. A moment of suspense, needless to say. At this moment of the day. On this particular day of the year. A year which is very special to us all on account of the Transfiguration which will occur as soon as sufficient numbers of us are persuaded, beyond all reasonable doubt, to live with the necessary degree of *concentrated fervour*. I hold out little hope for such an outcome. I observe in my perambulations too much slackness at the window – the careless raising up of cups to the lips as the eyes swivel to batten down upon a point of the most utter uselessness just beyond the surface of the table. Why can they not all be convinced to take life seriously, minute by minute, to subject it to analysis so acute and so mercilessly particular that nothing of true import will finally escape our attention? Call this if you like the babblings of an ugly, gout-afflicted stranger. Call this if you choose so to do a modicum of madness. Remember this though: I know what I know. Your tight little box is waiting just around the corner. You may wish to temper your flightiness.

The sea is known only for its heavings. I have never known the sea to sit perfectly still, in a well upholstered chair, for minutes together. I have never known the sea not to call back eagerly when called. The sea will have no truck with silence. Even when the night is ink-dark everywhere, and we lie there beneath the sheets, gently cowering, the sea is still murmuring for all its worth, restlessly turning in its bed, flinging up the rubbishy chit chat and chattels of millions. The sea, in short, is so disgusting that my latest plan – there is always something afoot in my life – is to drill a hole in its side and take pleasure in all that slow seepage.

The three of us, all old friends tried and trusted, came together one day – it was a day much like any other, or so we thought – in order to drive a smart, keen wedge between the months of August and October by creating SEPTEMBER. We had never admired that abrupt transition from mellow-skinned, toothy beach-babes to overmuch sludge, rain and cold. We gave it that name after the briefest and most off-hand of round-table discussions, and then we proceeded to create a profile, which began something like this: *season of mist and mellow fruitfulness*. It was then that the problems started – I should have known this from earlier rocky experiences in successful advertising agencies. Rocky hated mist. It made his shoulders quake and shiver just to think of them descending all of a sudden like a wet, damp felt cloak upon a scene perfectly idyllic until that moment. Roger hated the word *seasons* – let alone *season* – altogether. He had no belief in the crude compartmentalising of nature. The world should be encouraged to flow on in its customarily haphazard way, uninterruptedly, a source of perpetual pleasure and surprise. I tended to agree, although I said nothing just then because I have too often been accused of loosing off shafts of negativity. And yet, as you are aware, it happened all the same. When the idea leaked out, it became unstoppable. People actually loved it. Someone even finished the poem. Which means that we were stuck with it. And, what is worse, we had not even registered the patent, so it earned the three of us sweet F. A. That's a sharp lesson in life for all of us, I'm sure you'd agree.

This task may prove to be the equal of all too few... That is how the letter began, quite tentatively, and I pushed it along throughout the day, not knowing quite how it would be received. Or *when,* if the truth be known, it would be received. The various wigs were drying on the window sill, all arranged there seemingly at random. That situation could go on for days and days. It is important to take advantage of the good drying weather that we are enjoying. Freakish or not? One never knows quite how soon the wind might turn when one is faced with a sea quite as unpredictable as the Adriatic. The stillness of the lagoon is deceptive, always. I myself have lived in Venice all my life, and I would not have it otherwise. Life has always been a glittering masquerade. Many choose to disagree. Many leave of their own accord. Others are forced out. A fourth strain is rapidly incarcerated as if they were so much dross to brisk-sweep along the *calle* and then into the nearest canal. That is where my letter comes in, which has been so long in the drafting and the re-drafting. One must after all strike the right note, choose the *mot juste*, or all will be lost. I am a man who bides his time, who watches, and then takes a single step back, often into the shadow, because the shadow is always so cooling. You understand what I mean, don't you? It can be a bit of a rigmarole. At other times, it may smack of a dance step much to be admired. You choose how you look at me. Having said all that, I must on no account slacken in my efforts because I do feel for such men. There are those who were born at the wrong historical moment, whose loyalties are skewed by some unfair accident of history. Or some unfair accident perpetrated by man. My hand begins to tremble when I think again of such matters. I must distract myself. I must take a short perambulation in the direction of the Rialto. One or two may even smile at me. Or is it that my *bella donna* once again, she who must always walk in step with me?

We queued until Tuesday, and then we left off for a while. Gathered in groups to compare notes. Someone even pulled out packs off cards, several of them, which we spilled out onto the pavement, wantonly. Notes of hilarity were struck. Anything to stave off the boredom. Who exactly *were you* back there, I remember asking myself (without ever actually voicing the words because I did not finally really care, or not sufficiently), and why did you choose to join us anyway? It is surprising how few new ones do attach themselves to the cause, given that it has always been so self-evident. Nothing ever goes away, does it? What is more, the queue alone, day after day, *makes* it self-evident. Yes, it does tend to die away for a while, as if deflated, but then, yes, it always starts over again with that wearisome air of dogged inevitability. Then the light falters and someone, some self-appointed spokesperson of above medium height, gives the word, and we all, as one, roll out the body bags, and kip down for a day or two, seemingly without a care in the world, while the gulls wheel over us, idling, swooping, on the look out, I suppose, for random scraps of chip paper. There is always hope amidst such hopelessness. Was that your slogan? Everything belongs to everyone now. Or perhaps to no one, if you opt for the negative side of the coin. Flip it again then. Your choice, padre! I won't stop you. You're your own man, always have been. By dawn – or soon after – we are all it again, upright, dusting down right or left trouser leg, though without comment or conversation of any kind now. Could that be down to thirst or hunger? For whatever reason, elusive or no, this is what happens after days of queuing. All those once eager wishes to speak out quite drain away like pus from a suppurating wound. There is far too much of it all the time these days, with Nothingness hovering over. And I'm speaking generally. Don't try to tie me down to particularities. Thinking that you're so good at it doesn't mean that you are. It's at such times as this that I stare hard at you again, not really knowing whether I really know you at all. And after all these years! What were all those lumpish interludes called conversation really about then? Tell me. I won't be giving you my version of reality any time soon. The brass band, the tinkling cymbals… all so much phooey. Sad all the same. There used to be something in it, something small and perhaps even vibrant.

Every day it would happen. I wouldn't be able to sleep at nights – in fact, I dreaded the night's oncoming – because I would always know that it was about to happen. There was no need for it, we'd both agreed on that, but that doesn't mean that you didn't choose to make it happen – almost as if to defy me. Almost as if to ensure that there would never be anything smooth or easy-going about our relationship. You'd shake the bed and wake me, quite deliberately, swerving off to one side, and then bouncing and groaning, so loudly too! Anyone normal, anyone who did not bear an undeclared grudge against the world, would have had no compulsion to do such a thing.

I'd drive myself up onto my elbow and say what I always said. After all, what else was there to say? You don't have to do it! I'd shout out to you. You'd be bent over on the side of the bed, almost falling off. You don't have to go! They are not expecting you! I'd see you frantically finger-combing your hair, giving yourself time to muster all your enmity against me. Of course I do! You'd blurt out like some mad thing. Of course they are expecting me! Then – it's always the same miserable routine – you'd shoot your wrist watch out of its ragged, unbuttoned cuff, and dangle it in front of my face, as if to prove the truth of all your nonsense. What truth is there in a watch? I ask you. Who ever sought or found truth in a watch! See what hour it is! you'd say, banging the watch face against my chest. It's half past two, and it starts at three! Even if I were to run, I would barely make it. Stop! I'm shouting back now. Stop this! There's no place like that down the street, no factory any more. I'm shouting at the top of my voice. You're cowering now. You fall to the floor. Shouting like that's the only thing to do, the only way to stop it happening. That place beside the river disappeared twenty years ago! I go on, voice rising to a sepulchral shriek. We watched it together, being dynamited. We took a half bottle of whisky down there. We held hands when the tower fell. It was quite some thrill really, almost a social thing, for the two of us. There were others chinking bottles too! And anyway, – it's at this point that I drag you back onto the bed; you're like a limp, blubbering dishrag by now – you were never cut out to be a nightwatchman, with your pathetic physique and your nerviness! For Christ sake, give us both a break, Gerald!

There was a sign just above the door that I could never quite read. Too many people had scratched at it with their nails in fury; too many filthy boys had leant back and doused it with their fierce, climbing jets of urine. I knew that I would feel sad, now and forever more, to see it so neglected. I wanted it to be bright-shining and new again. I wanted it to be painted as I remember it to have once been painted. I wanted to burst through that door and shout out some greeting to someone who would be listening out for me. On the other hand, it was an entirely useless endeavour, I was quite aware of that too. What is the point of re-painting a door sign above a door when there was no door there any more? And no house either. Why was I even going there? Just to look? Just to be reminded of how much vanishes when you are not paying attention? How could I have been looking anyway? I hear you asking. I didn't even live in these parts any more. I'd even forgotten the language. Anyway, some compulsion kept me there on that miserable spot for hours at a time. I even told the cab driver to go away and eat something in a cafe – if he could find a cafe in these parts. Nothing was as it once had been – no street signs, no people, no nothing. Just those lazily rising spirallings of dust and all that flatness stretching away. Only the rain would settle the dust. I decided to pick up the sign anyway, even though I could barely bring myself to touch it. It was like an amulet to me. It seemed to burn in my hand. I would re-paint it myself. I would teach myself the meaning of the word again as I worked on it in my studio. I would paint it in firm red capital letters and hang it above my own door to see whether it held as much meaning there as it once did above the old door. There is so much meaning to be lost and found in the simple heartbreak of a word like HOME.

I took the one word, deliverance, and I tried to breathe new life into it by uttering it over and over again, first of all in this room, and then out in the street, at the crossroads over yonder, where the trucks take a blind turn at such lightning speed. I wanted deliverance to feel as if it were made for me again, as if I alone had conjured it into being because of some profound need to make it work for me. There had been other words in the past, words about which my very being seemed to pivot, but nothing quite like deliverance. I had only the vaguest of notions of what exactly I wanted to be delivered from – or, indeed, whether I wanted to be delivered at all. It couldn't be death, that ultimate human experience, because when I touched my warm body I found that I was still very much alive, and sometimes even in the throes of singing, to my heart's content. So I had no inclination to be delivered from a death experience because death seemed not to be willing its own oncoming. Did I wish to be delivered from this family which had dutifully fed and nurtured me then? I looked at them one by one that evening – an old, crabbed, grouchy man stooped over the stove; that woman I called my mother, who spent her daylight hours looking out for life's long since vanished opportunities just beyond the window; and this sister of mine, who never spoke a word to me because her glorious life was always streaming ahead of her... Did I need them any more? Would deliverance's sweet tune beguile me away forever if I could only make it come alive for me? What then was preventing me from saying it with any true conviction?

I found a city, the broad outspreading of a place fine-stitched and threaded with light, in a valley more marvellous than anything I had ever seen in my young life, even before I had located my very own small hole to nest in. I know I needed such a hole, but it had never been there for me. Nor had nakedness – the nakedness of the womb, for example. I had slithered out into the world fully clothed, and at such a giddying rate. From the beginning, from that first in-taken breath and on, I was standing upright, and even walking at speed onward, onward, even before I had learned to blink awake like a helpless babe, and acknowledge everything that circled round about me, the wonder of it all. I knew nothing of wonder. All I knew was of this need to move ahead, looking out, at all times, to left and to right of me, looking out for those snipers with their whiplash tongues, those who would do me down. So I hit on a solution to it it all, this dilemma of my life. I would pretend to be hopeless, helpless, and so I fell to my knees, giggling, red-faced, and as I squirmed around in the dirt, I began to drag off my shirt, my trousers. Soon enough I was writhing there naked, and even though I felt them standing over me, and breathing all their filthy breath into my face, I prayed, I knew, as if by some unerring instinct, that they would never have the gall even to touch me, let alone molest me, let alone tear me limb from limb. And so I slept at last, peacable enough.

Her name is Mona. She cannot go by any other name because that is the name I have bequeathed to her. No, I have not told her. I did not need to tell her. I did not need to speak to her at all. In fact, it was far better that I should not speak to her, that I should keep my distance from her, because I had no wish to know of the messy and disgusting particularities of her life, what soup she slurped, how she pulled on her scratchy stockings, how often she yawned for no good reason at all. None of that was to the point. The point resided in her name – Mona – as though in some beauteous casket, and all that it gave me, of an instant, even when the rain drums down on this roof as it does now, without even having to be asked. It all came skipping along one day as I slept the sleep of the enviable. I saw her there, that girl, so much better than she had ever been. And I, I was better too. I stood upright, with a look of assurance on my face. I did not cough in the way that I habitually do. I did not spread my coins out on the table with the kitchen curtains drawn, pushing them back and forth. Counting, counting, forever counting. I merely kept them in my pocket, quite discreetly, and only occasionally ran them through my fingers. And as she came by in front of me, I dropped her the most coy of sidelong smiles, not over-eager in any way, not desperate to claw at her flesh like some street cat, and she too, she looked so modest in her turn, and she dropped me such a look of restraint, but it was a restraint which went hand in hand with a small and secret pledge to be with me by and by, I knew that. And with that assurance, I crept back home, and I communed with myself about Mona, and her abiding loveliness and dependability.

This is life's moment, I know that for a fact. I do not need to be told any more. Once upon a time, I would have waited for them to tell me. I would have hung back. I would have hesitated. I would have deemed myself insufficient to be so knowing. Too small, too singular, too little formed perhaps. Now I am wholly within the steadfast grip of myself, and of this moment here too, which I declare now to be life's moment. No matter that this room is at it is, dirty, ramshackle, of the kind that no one would envy. No matter that I am who or what

I am. Am I a who or a what? you might ask. I am a little of either, a little of both. Or a little of neither. And yet now I am enough of a man to know this to be my life's moment. When I step out of doors, the entire sky seems to frame me, clouds curtsy, the winds cool me, the rain refreshes me, the traffic lights wink fondly at me, dogs accompany me for a block or two in order to be seen with me. What more could I ask than this? I do not need to speak to anyone. The need for speech, the need to explain myself to the experts, has all quite fallen away. I am who I am, and you are who you are, and you must accept that this will remain the case forever. I have done quite enough budging, quite enough shilly-shallying in my life.

What words did you use when you spoke? Any? Many? You certainly mouthed a few, perhaps silently, perhaps under your breath, in my direction. Am I mistaken then? No, I am not mistaken. Were you not over there just then, beyond that heap of rosaries? I knew that I knew you, that I recognised you from my childhood. There was something about your lips, and even something about the way that you stooped to pick up... What did you pick up? What did you cup in your hand, rather coyly? I knew those gestures through and through. And then you had gone again, as quickly as you came, and I am left here now groping to find you. I do not know why the light of you is fading so quickly within me. It was so bright just moments again. It was almost as if we had been married twice over, such was our intimacy as I stared at you over there, in all your customary finery, which even then looked as if it might once have been some other's because it did not hang too well about your person. Did I care about any of that? No, I most certainly did not. There was a certain sweetness about your awkwardness. I had this urge – and just now too! – to embrace you for it. But I cannot do that now because there is no you hereabouts to embrace any more, not even in memory. That heap of rosaries has dissolved into nothingness too. Why so many? Were they all yours? Had they been abandoned? Did no one care any more, about that sight of you over there, perhaps letting slip a word or two in my direction, and those rosaries just beyond, which must surely once have belonged to someone?

You always called this a town like no other. I didn't see it like that. I looked at the town, and I saw where it ended, where the scrubland began, and how few of us there were in the bar, always, always the same bitter few, and indeed so tragically few that within a matter of minutes we had come to the end of all topics of conversation. I would ask them, I would shout it out loud: why so few? Why not more? Why don't others join us? What a hoaxer I am! My life is full of pretence. I knew why well enough, though I didn't say, and I do believe that we all knew why. How could we not? I didn't dare – none of us dared – to declare the miserable consequences of the fact that we were all there to indulge a shared passion for the music of the eleven-stringed dulcimer. The dulcimer itself was not to blame. It was a blameless object of beauty, one of its kind, manufactured in a workshop in the proud mountains of Kentucky by our forefathers so long ago that merely to be forced to think back to that day, when it was borne on their shoulders down from the mountain, brought on the most terrible spasms of collective weeping. It was our greatest treasure, our only treasure, and it lived with us at the price of isolation. Yes, that dulcimer was also our curse, I tell you, because the wood from which it was fashioned was kept supple and unharmed by the liberal daily application of one timeless product only: skunk juice. And what sequestered rural community could possibly prosper or expand or feel well of itself when it is at the mercy of vats a-brim with skunk juice?

I would never declare that my own mother is in the grip of religious mania. I would never tell anyone how many hours she spends kneeling beside her bed, muttering her inaudible prayers, and even occasionally gnashing her teeth and wailing over her manifold sins. We creep in at such times. We stroke her back. We finger-comb her matted hair. We kiss her tear-dampened cheeks. We endeavour to console her for what she regards as her lifelong shortcomings, but she is not to be consoled. In fact, she barely registers our presence there at all. I would never write of the notes that she leaves for us, her many, many children, propped beside packets of dry, uncooked foodstuffs. We love her too much to tell the authorities that she neglects us, that she fails to provide for us. In fact, in our heart of hearts, we do not truly believe that she does neglect us. We regard her instead as the embodiment of holiness, like some great and shining monument to be revered, albeit a tragic one for which we also feel a measure of pity. It is for this reason that after her prayerful wrestlings are over and done, we lead her to the table and sit her down, and give her the hot food that we have cooked for her, spooning it into her mouth as she mumbles and mutters inconsolably, like some wrecked thing who knows that, though on the shoreline now, she will never truly be rescued because there will always be those greater waves oncoming by and by, all waiting to engulf her.

She has said no such thing. We have listened, and there has been nothing but silence. We have checked, repeatedly. We have been in and out of her cell, like a great wave washing back and forth, that regular, that dependable. And there has been nothing from her. Not a creak, Not a squeak. She sits there slumped over, as she must always sit. We have not imposed it upon her, this posture of hers. She herself declared that it would be so, and it has been so ever since she made that declaration. She would never presume to rise so high again, being so lowly now. She understands the consequences, the manifold consequences, of her actions, and she has agreed that muteness is to be the way. We have burnt everything that she had, everything that once made her great amongst us, the finery, the props (so flimsy), and even the contents of her extensive armoury. All gone. All committed to the flames. We felt so proud to see it all go, rising to the sky in a great spiralling of grey smoke, grey on grey, as some noticed and remarked for our general edification. It was as if we were seizing hold of our own lives again, growing into our true selves, that which we had always meant to be, and had not quite become until that moment of exquisite reckoning. Is it quite enough though? We have asked each other that question in many plenary sessions, over and over again we have asked it, the very same question, though sometimes slightly differently expressed in order not to bore ourselves too much. And after asking that question, we have all gone again to look at her, marching in single file up to her, one behind another, dolefully, being fully aware of the potential gravity of the situation. And then, one by one, we have all squinted through the rusting metal grill, and contemplated the sad wizenedness, the miserable shrunkenness, of her current situation. We have considered how far she has fallen, like a great bird which has plummeted down, down from the sky, spectated at in awe and wonderment by those proud bearers of guns. Anger? Pity? Renewed spasms of vengefulness? Each one of us, each in our turn, is subject to all of these emotions, in differing degrees, at different hours of the day or the night. The ball is tossed up high in the air. We watch it fall, and are consumed by wonderment and perplexity.

The keeper of the lock lives in a cottage whose identity is not widely known to us. We like it to be like that. We live in horror of casual tourism. We do not encourage onlookers or overlookers of any kind. We are sufficient unto ourselves. The keeper of the lock is more than sufficient unto himself. We do not ask him how he cares for it, whether he has rags, tools for twisting and probing and tweezering, the appropriate oils of lubrication. We trust him to look after it, appropriately. Similarly, we ourselves never ask to see it. Why should we, being who we are, mere day-labourers, knowing nothing of darker or deeper things – things of the night, for example? What business would it be of ours to snoop so on a thing quite so sacred? It would demean us. It would also make a mockery of its character. It would transform it, as if by the wave of a wand, into some casual thing, casual to handle, casual to contemplate. It is no such thing. We saw it once, when the town's gates were flung back, and that once was more than sufficient. It remains there as it must, beyond the reach of all of us, to our greater good, you must understand – if you are capable of understanding anything.

The leap must not be taken lightly because the depths down into the chasm of the Falls, my goodness me... All this is truly unknowable. Most of all to be emphasised is the superabundant beauty of the scene, and how the rolling mist appears to hang over at the very point where it plunges down, in all its majestic immensity. We love it, let me emphasise that fact, we love it more than we love any other feature of this place because it is such a challenge to us all. We are so small beside it. It is so large. What is more, it possesses such musculature, such a power to overwhelm and overawe. It puts one in the mood for sacrifice without a doubt. The difficulty is who is to be sacrificed, who deserves to be singled out in this way. That is why I began by speaking of the dangers of the frivolous impulse, and how that frivolity is not to be indulged. Youth, for example, is subject to such whims. If we were to encourage a leap by the entire community, both young and old, on the other hand, that might be a better way of proceeding, because then we would all be as one, and such a sacrifice on such a scale would resonate globally. How could it not? Although this township would then be bereft of all human resources, who would not then flock to it in order to wonder and to marvel? What human being on this earth would not fall to his knees in acknowledgment of how we had all risen as one, and so magnificently, to the stupendous challenge of all that incessant roaring?

I should, like, above all things else, for everything to remain as it is. That would be the most satisfactory state of affairs. As soon as there is any movement to the left or the right of me, re-consideration follows, almost inevitably, in its wake, and there emerges by and by a general agitation, a general dislike of things as they are, a haphazard yearning of sorts – for no one ever knows quite when or where – to change them. That must not happen. That must not be allowed to happen. Let all things remain as they are today in this world, perfectly somnolent, with the slow movement of cattle across the plains, and the odd inchoate mewling of a child in its cot, hoisted up high behind the gantry. Who would wish to change any of that? Who would wish to change the way that he looks, for example, the resigned blandness hereabouts, to put on a mask of anger or perplexity? None of us, not a one, wants any of that. Here each one of us sits on the edge of the bed, head dutifully bowed in homage to the peaceable state of things, as the sallow yellow of dawnlight breaks like an egg upon us. Nobody utters a word. There is perfect silence in this kingdom. How could it be otherwise? I hear you say. That day when all our tongues were ripped out, it was a day of shocking cruelty, granted. It was a day that so many regretted because they remembered the mellifluousness of particular tender young voices. It was also a day when wisdom was imposed upon us, as if from above, as if by the application of an iron rod. It was also good for us. All random yearnings have passed away. The study of such contentment as we have, and how it is eked out daily, is now our solemn duty.

She leaped so high that morning that no one felt inclined to speak about it later. In a single mighty bound she cleared the General Savings Bank on Main Street, even giving an insouciant finger-twirl to the weathervane as she skimmed over it. We opted instead for other topics of conversation – how the traffic was shaping up down the highway this morning, for example, on a day of low skies such as this one. It seemed fitting to ignore her. It seemed the right thing to do. Her growth had troubled us for months: her growth, her strength, her general stridency when she walked or lounged or cavorted about the streets. We loved her in our own very particular way, of course. She was one of ours. We had named her. We would never disown her. We also continued to watch her closely. We monitored, that was the official parlance, which brought about a degree of aggravation on her part. She would look at us as if she did not belong to us any more. We reminded her of our names, and of all that she had shared with us. We pointed to her father in his backyard over yonder, who was deep-hoeing just then, driving that back-hoe in so deep, and with such a nervy determination, that no man could have been his equal. See that man amongst men? we said to her, pointing, as if addressing a fool's horse. I see nothing but good dirt flying where it must, and in an arc quite as wide as it is high, she remarked – a characteristically withering riposte to which, in the end, we gave no finely calculated response at all.

I am pointing to myself as I say it! All this is music, all that I am telling you today, all these flights of fancy, all these soarings above and across, all these plungings down and sudden upward soarings. That is why I am moving so lightly on my toes in my ravishing silver heels because, being the now deathless embodiment of the spirit of music, I barely touch down at all. You tell me that you do not hear me, that my voice does not reach you, that you do not even see me when I walk in front of you, no matter who or what musical motif I may choose to resemble. You even deny that I am your first born, your only son. You tell me that you have lost me, and that you do not know how to find me again. You even deny that you have fabricated something quite so wondrous as this marvellous, nigh-on evanescently otherworldly thing that I am still in the throes of becoming. And even when I appear in front of you, you screw up your eyes against me as if everything that I am is abhorrent to you. Let me lift you up now and dance with you. Let me lift the sad sack of you up, up into the air, with all your groans and your denials and your endless weepings for every way in which you have failed me, and shake you about violently like a medicine in a bottle, and then shout into your face that you have not failed me because I am who I am today, and every day I am a little more of myself. You will simply have to get used to it.

The coarseness is all about the lips, the teeth, the gums, the general letting go. He is not to be blamed for all of this, of course. One day his arms swung down, and then remained as they were, entirely motionless for the most part until a passing wind chose to blow on them a little, causing them to stir, which quite surprised him when it happened. He looked. He looked away. He looked. Otherwise, what is to be done? We could prop him somewhere convenient to us all, somewhere between here and there, for example, before or after one of the irregular feedings. We could even align him with the stars in some fashion yet to be determined, for the greater good luck of us all. Such things have been done before without dire consequences. There is no denying that he is both a burden and a hazard, and that we heartily wish him away. But he will not go away, not of his own accord. Every morning, he is stubbornly present once again. Does he not wake us with his roarings from the barn? Does he not rattle the shackles, as if somehow he is underserving of such treatment? Well, he may well have forgotten by now, but we have not forgotten. We have not forgotten how, one evening, just when a tipsy interlude of the most delicate kind was supervening, he stepped down from his pedestal and began to swing to left and to right with the utmost recklessness, as if he had the authority to impose upon us in this way. Had he been a father, we might have begin to comprehend, but being who he was, this drifter of a man with the vilely shrunken gums, we were disinclined to listen to his message. I have no idea at all. Do winds come bearing auguries? Yours to reply if and when you feel so inclined.

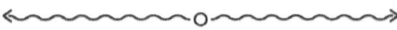

The skeleton of a donkey, surely. Thoroughly scarified and then left here, flung beside the road, as if bearing some message. Not a thing to be much heeded, and so we hurry along. My donkey, on the other hand, I pamper it with fistfuls of hay pushed at the churning pink gums. And then: such brays! Such brays! To listen to the mood of a market garden such as this one demands the talents of a necromancer. Fortunately, I am such a man. I am also a sea captain. Correction: I have been a sea captain in my time – Madeira to the Azores, quite that far flung. Now? Now I am beached and contented. The world of my carrots, my sunflowers, my lettuces, it all pivots about me. When I rise, I feel it in my bones, the gift, the low, contented hum of my centrality. Even my wife is inclined to look at me askance, though fondly. We have grown like two trees, sky thrusters, plucky. Yes, even my wife comes bearing a modicum of respect for me when she also transports the lettuces. What else is there to be done? The beetroot cocks a ready ear. The basil knows when to spring its freshness. The sun too makes amends for its absence in the spring by gifting me and mine – and yours and ours! – with a summer such as this one. Why then that scarified donkey just then, as if flung down to taunt me?

I would not have you enquire of such an outcome. I would set it aside with the one word: hush. Or perhaps a *hush-a-bye,* stolen from the nursery, where they all must lie a-sleeping, forever. Were you there with me? Or did I travel alone? I remember the station, and how the train hushed – that word again! – along beside the platform, with such stealth. I boarded – the only one. (Who travels at such an hour?) I was in a teeming hurry. I failed to enquire the destination. Any destination would do. I would be free again! Even the suitcase had been forgotten. It was a wonder that I was wearing any clothes at all. I merely sat there and looked out. The nothingness of it all stared back at me, the superabundance of choices, none yet quite taken, and then, when it began to leave (without prompting, needless to say), a general thrill rose up within me. It was as if it knew that it was bearing me away, and when we entered the tunnel, the train and I together, there was such collusion between us, such depths of darkness into which, momentarily plunging, I almost lost myself! And after? Well, what is there to say? I lived my life much like any other. Cards from the pack, one laid down after another. Betrayals were few. There were consequences, inevitably. And I grew to adore that spot where land meets sea because I knew that just there I could step off and be anyone, anywhere. I never did, of course. Better not to be chased. Better to hide here in plain view and pretend that so little has happened.

I said yes one time too many. Yes! Yes! Yes! They were looking out for it. They were counting. There were only so many yeses to be allotted. Optimism must be rationed. And so I fell dumb. For hours I said nothing. I slithered my feet around in order to distract myself. But I was not distracted. My brain was working, churning, churning, like an over-fed stomach. Something had to give. So I spat them forth: no, no, no, no. The sky darkened to an inky black. I held my composure. I neither blinked nor blenched. We all looked towards the window in acknowledgement of the impact of my words of decision. There was a general easing off, a mood of careless congratulation, a slapping of backs, a drawing forth of cigarettes. And then it happened at last, to tumultuous applause, the falling of the bombs, that almighty blessing.

<hr>

It was the day of her arrival again, the same day, and yet another day altogether, because I had failed to recognise her this time around. Everything about her was different, to the extent that she was a different woman altogether, surely. I was almost wholly convinced of it, the proportions, the height, that lilt of hers when she chose to speak, which was seldom. I even asked her. I presented myself in front of her, somewhat obsequiously, like a gift on a platter, wrapped and presented for a very special occasion. Was this a special occasion? I found myself asking myself, as if I might have been addressing any passing stranger. Special or not? Same day or not? Same woman or not? The words were rattling around inside my head like peas in a box, any old box, and any number of peas, hard or soft, large or of middling size. Was this not after all another day, a day much like any other, with the usual wall between us and them, and the usual gouts of bad breath from just beyond the wall, seeping through intermittently, as it tended to do, on that kind of a day? Or on *this* kind of a day, to be a tad more precise? And there she was, wholly present to me! And yet was that glance of hers not somewhat askance after all, as if she had just caught the eye of one who was standing just behind me, a little to the left of me perhaps, but still undeniably behind me? Should I wheel around, and thereby embarrass her by an act which would surely be widely regarded as accusatory? Yes, would that gesture cause her to think that I was accusing her of ignoring me? Or should I go the whole hog and ignore her altogether, having quietly concluded that I was not entirely present to her, not vividly present, that is, not an object (or perhaps a someone) that she was eager to behold after all? Well, how puzzling this was all proving to be! I even, somewhat resignedly, somewhat world-wearily it has to be said, sat down at the table and took up the water glass again. I had to do something about this enormous lump that was rising in the throat, somewhat as water on a flood plain rises and rises without even so much as asking. I was worried about that lump. Were it to continue to rise and to rise, I would be prevented in the fulness of time from speaking altogether. This was, needless to say, not a subject I could ever raise with her, being far too personal and particular to myself. Were I even to hint at its existence, and explain to her, no matter how briefly, how ominous I regarded it, she would snatch up a book from this table top, this very same table top, and quickly turn a page, and then another. I knew that would happen. I knew what sort of a woman she was. I was not blind to her disadvantages. I had seen round the back of her on more than one occasion. Perhaps even two – if numbers are a part of this game.

Numbers fly off and away. Nothing to be done. Nothing to be said. What would be the use of it anyway, talking to numbers, conversing with numbers? They do not talk back. They cannot. They have no voice boxes to speak of. They have no wherewithal to be anything but numbers, mute and solemn and dumb and still, laid down flat in their patterns, their regular or irregular patterns, or wheeling around in the air from, time to time, in dreamtime, that is, in order to be perfect torments to me. Why is it that they taunt me in this way? Who put them up to it? What malevolence pointed them down such a path? It all started off so easily, so painlessly. There were the house numbers along this street, for example, evens on the left, unevens on the right. Plain as the best of rainless spring days. Piercing blue as the sky on a clear spring morning. That simple. And then, by and by, without warning or ceremony, they began to lift away. They began to play their teasing little games with me. They began to rearrange themselves. Not one and then three and then five and then seven, but seven and then nineteen and then twenty-seven. My head began to heat like a kettle coming to the boil. I was obliged to sit down all of a sudden. I could make nothing of anything any more. I was being carried. I was being set aside. I was being poured into a sack. I myself was being counted, finger-sifted, one by one, and then by twos and threes and ever odder ones.

It is not wholly unreasonable of me to chance upon this gate again. The question is a simple one: how many gates are there in total anyway in this life of ours, and what would be the likelihood of my standing here now, on a day such as this one, bucket firmly in hand, and buoyed by a mood of near preternatural excitement? Play it as you will, it is almost bound not to go away because too much attention is being paid to it already, and when overmuch attention is lavished, the object does tend to linger. It is the way of things. No one forces this life along. You could even say that we are helpless to prevent it anyway. Hole in bucket. Sand streaming through. That sort of thing. Depressing perhaps — were it not also exhilarating in so far as it keeps us in the mood. Like rats scampering hell-for-leather through sewers. Five-bar, that is the extent of it, no more than a child's gate, though the child in question would need to be plucky and substantial, as the newer children tend to be. You get my drift about that one. I myself am wholly indifferent to the matter. I stand to one side, as if at a bus stop. Waiting. Patiently waiting. Never boarding. Too hazardous by half. I am at my most casual on, say, a Thursday, when I have a half-day, and everything is footloose, and gates seem like exactly the thing to do. Would you come too? Are you of a mind for such an adventure? Do you even like them? Would you eat them if there were to be this sudden absence of food — which is, of course, always being threatening? I built one once. Not this one. You reminded me of one. But that was yesterday. Our friendship need not suffer. Unless you pull away. Idle threats are the day's stock-in-trade. We don't have to agree on anything.

There is this untidy, unruly mishmash going on — or so they say. You swung down from the attic, monkey-wise, and threw me such a look that I was rooted to the spot until the clock struck nine or ten or thereabouts. Have it your way, I say. Why not say it though? Who else would speak up for me now? Not, surely, all those graveyard ones, such old grumps the lot of them. Better left to lie. Then you left me. Having faced me down in the kitchen doorway, and after a single spiky glower, you left me. It was as simple as that. I have had quite enough and more, that's what you said, quickly and crisply, as any good woman might. And then you made that rid-of-you gesture with your hands, quick-dusting palms together, as if rubbing off all the bread flour that remained. I understood all right. I knew what you meant. You also left all your things, choking up everywhere. I called after you: you've left all your things! I shouted. I rose to this shouty occasion. No need to make it all so street-welcoming, Gobby, you shouted back as you hurried on towards the only bus stop in this village, and that too under threat. Through the mist of the abundance of my crocodile tears, it was as if you were melting away like any homely pat of new churned butter in full view of the morning's fat sunlight streaming in through the kitchen window on a day of the cherished kind that we used to have together, before we got to know each other so thoroughly that we became utterly intolerable to each other. That is the word I need to cling to. Otherwise, it is much the same as ever. When you were here you were not here. When I was here with you, I was not here with you. We were going about our various things with more than a modicum of brisk aggression. Now the light falls slowly beyond and behind the municipal car park, and I find myself so currently possessed by the peace and the sweet good reasonableness of it all that I opt to do nothing whatsoever but watch it.

He asked for far, far more than he was given. He asked several times. He projected his arms straight out from his body, palms fully open and extended, expectant of manna or such like. Nothing. Sweet nothings. The sky seemed full of the usual heady promise – no resistance there. The ground beneath his feet was level enough. He could walk ahead on his own two legs, he supposed, were he to choose so to do. Nothing in this respect had changed. The mechanism of the body was fully charged, fully lubricated. Why go anywhere though? Why expect anything different elsewhere? Why not everything here and now? What would be the point of budging when the much that was to be resolved seemed to demand an immediate... what exactly though? His rags too – thin, if not papery – were much as they always had been. Flapping out to left and to right of him when the wind troubled to stir, seemingly in acknowledgment of his singular presence there. Seldom. He could see once again the man walking towards him, the man who always came walking towards him when he was in the grip of a mood such as this one, a man who resembled himself to a quite uncanny degree. And yet all the same he did *not* quite resemble him. The attitude, for example, was profoundly different. There was a nonchalant swagger about him, and even a careless kicking out of the legs. He was narrow-eyed, quite cynically so, appearing both to see and not to see. Even when waved at, brightly or eagerly, he never responded. And at the point of arrival, he veered off to such an extent that when he looked up, he would be approaching all over again from the same direction, yes, he would be steadily oncoming from that very same distance away, a barely discernible pin prick at first. And so he stood there once again, as he so often had done, thinking this, with thought itself idling like some engine ticking over: there could perhaps be worse outcomes than this one. This one at least is a pardonable distraction.

There came a river between, a furious, fast-flowing river, which now divided one from another. A general bewilderment. An overwhelming anger, with arms flung out, and bellowings and furious stampings back and forth, all to no avail. No river budges at the request of a mere man, no river has second thoughts. The thoughts amongst men were all of means to an end: sacrifice, of course! Having flung in the eldest, they watched him sink. The river surged on. The river is a heartless space, on that they were all agreed. Then a child began to sing his small and careless, carefree little song, with a tune that frisked and frolicked along, moving in no particular direction. And as the child walked back and forth along the river bank, singing, singing, the river too surged back and forth, as if catching at, and even being appeased somewhat, by the rhythm of that child's so dear singing. And in the fulness of time, the child knelt down and put his hand on the river to still it, and, lo, the river was stilled, and it was getting smaller by the minute. The thirsty river was drinking itself down to the dregs.

I would say that this is a statement being painfully born. Out with it. Out with it. *The genesis of it all* is its subject, as weighty, as cumbersome as that. I hear a squawk from the wings. Who can be doing with such things when we are off on a spree again? Less of that. In fact, all are standing here – such patience! – waiting to board, or at the very least to be at one with, the statement of a lifetime, which must, I have been warned, consist of an adequate summary. After all that's gone on! A lifetime of baggy and unwieldy things, from the fallings away to the tight graspings close, and everything in between. I was present at it all, you see. (Do you see?) That is why I have been invited to summarise it all. In a single sentence if possible. Pithy and to the point. With no small measure of wit as an aid to wakefulness. That sort of thing. You get the gist. I measure myself. Am I up to it? Have I seen so far? No matter. If I do not strike, now, who will? Who possesses the gall, the daring, the spunk at such an hour as this one? The boots are ready. I pull them on. Thigh-high when all the heaving's over and done. I settle the mouth, the eye. I raise the pen. Off then, off and away... It has written itself! In a jiff, no time at all! See it here. Read it at your leisure. Thanks are wholly beside the point. You would have done the same, had you been called on.

We spread the cans, in the thinnest of thin and wavering lines, up the edges of the street, the fresh-painted cans, in shiny blue, yellow, green, the old paint cans newly refurbished, freshly beautified, one by one by one, for this moment. How happy we were then! There is no moment more brim full of meaning than the moment of anticipation. We looked at each other with such pride. All that sourness had gone, all those shadows lifted off and away. Never had we looked so youthfully expectant. Certainly never in the days of our long gone youthfulness. From somewhere just behind the barns, tootlings and raspings and blarings and hummings were going on, which made us smile. Who would have guessed that all the old instruments, the ones that our grandfathers and grandmothers had played to their heart's content when the dam was still under construction, would have been plucked out of the hessian sacks again, and pressed into service? Who would have guessed that our very own children, those knock-kneed louts, those scruffy yobs, to a girl and a man, would have learnt how to play them, and even taken pleasure in so doing? Who could have guessed at such bonding at the end of a year of no holds barred catastrophe? Who might be thanked for such clemency? There were no ready contenders amongst us and so, for the most part, we remained steadfastly silent as we contemplated our various options.

This river is what you make of it. You cannot even guess at its colour (that slick surface sheen, for example), because any choice you might make is given the lie when the light chooses to fall in a certain way: on a grey morning such as this one, for example, when I find myself once again pacing back and forth beside it needless to say, trying to fathom its underlying meanings, or to take its measure. Rod and plumb line are perfectly useless. It vomits them forth. It yields up nothing. It stares above my head or looks behind me. Never back at me. The river never directly confronts me or challenges me with a message of any meaning or import. Is this a problem for my state of mind? Does it trouble or rattle me to be so treated by a river, which, in all honesty, has neither the tongue with which to speak nor the eyes with which to see? It is a matter of perfect indifference to me. The fact that I find myself here daily is a habit of which I could so easily rid myself, were I to choose so to do.

Into the habit of seeing again, clear-seeing that is, without the customary mist inserting itself between. Here is a land fit for me and mine for sure, a golden land, bright shining and ready, with every neighbours' applause rising up and up from the valley's bottom. And then it all dies away, and I fall into a slough of despond, dragging boots and more through valley, across streams, and up and down and then again and on to nowhere that I know in particular until I reach your door, on which I steadfastly hammer. Do I make myself hear? There you are inside, at your window seat, poking over atlas and map, preparing for a future. I make exaggerated mouthings, at which you lock the shutters − bang! − and turn up the music. I begin to dig the ditch of a lifetime, around the house and on, making it deeper and deeper, giving you such a fine and fast growing green perimeter that no one will ever know by and by who lives within with such towering aspirations. Does it bother you at all? Not at all. You take the watering can to it from the roof, standing there, poised and perfectly balanced, in all the majesty of your nakedness, spueing it forth in fine, high arcs, as you sing and sing to your soul's content.

Am I contented though? Or would I shove the parts around and about, and back and forth, and re-configure it all? Would I have this dark roof hanging over and louring so, this road roaring between my legs, this high heaven above me with its perennial nuisance of blinking stars to keep me awake when I would be contentedly snoring? Is that what I am to be? Is this what you are to remain, world? Should I not go indoors and close the door? Why wake up to it all again? Why be such a bother to myself and others? Why not remain down here lying, straight as a die, on this floor, as I have been for years now, barely breathing at all, not wishing to disturb? Is all this wrong or right? Am I not to rise up in the night with a clatter and a roar and shake the stuffing out of them all? Am I inclined to bother?

Will not all your gentle singing still suffice me, as it has done for years and years, seeping up through the floor, where you have so long been lying in all the contentment of your utter stillness, as I have listened and listened and listened, and given such thanks through my tears?

We dug down deep that day, all of us together, knowing that it had to be, that there was no alternative to all this laboursome digging, that it was our lot, our itch, our grievance, our final destination. And then, by and by, we stopped, and yanked out the bottles from the box, and drank and drank until we fell where we stood. We were so happy to fall, laughing and laughing, on that spot where we had been standing, beside those great holes we had been digging, and some of us even, the careless ones, those devil-may-care ones who had drunk so far beyond all caring, even fell where they had been digging, and knew nothing of the aftermath because no one could find them to tell them. And their names no longer clung to us.

A. I felt such pity when I saw you.

B. It was because I pitied *you*. It was nothing to do with how I looked *before* I pitied you. It was all down to you, and all your miserable poverty of conviction. How hang-dog you looked that morning as you stood at the door, waiting, panting for anything that I would toss in your direction. Confess it now. You are nothing but a small, whimpering dog, never have been otherwise.

A. That day, when I rose up like a rampant lion at your door, that was my best of moments, when you looked at me then in all my majesty and even inclined a little towards me.

B. It was all that hilarity at your expense, nothing else, that caused me to stumble when I saw you, dressed up in your moth-eaten lion's pelt, bought for next to nothing from some village jumble sale or other. How in heaven's name could you ever believe that such a look would win me?

A. I won you. You were my prize on that sultry and unpromising morning. I seized hold of you and carried you away to the hay loft, where I had my way with you from that day forth.

B. Yes, you asked me to sew up all the holes, I remember, after my sniggers had died away, and we finally exchanged a few civil words with each other. I told you I was not a seamstress, that I had only ever been a lonely biker on the freeways, and that you would have to settle for that.

A.B. *And we settled for that.*

The paltry light shone forth one morning, a December day. A thin scrim of ice on the wrong side of the window, distorting all our seeing out. You had left already, and I was just about to leave too, because there was nothing else for it. We had had that concluding conversation. And now it was as if nothing had happened. I am talking about all this numbness within, of how we leave and then arrive again and then leave again, as if it is someone else doing it all, within the vacancy of our two lives together. Two? Only two? Who has been counting? Do you feel anything? Have you ever? Walking together can be such a small thing in the absence of solid conversation. Walking together then, two phantom selves making such intricate moves, as if the entire world consists of all this careful counting before we dare do anything else. Would you say that you are contented? I was reaching back just now to find whatever it is that I had lost, and that was oh so long ago, some foolish childhood thing that finally meant so much. Why though? How could it, when it is so long gone? And who were you then anyway? Such a small creature, surely, and of such little consequence. Marks on a board, all rubbed out. This is perhaps the little that I expect of myself when I am not snatching at the moon and the stars. And now you are back here again, of course, in the customary chair beside the fire, staring ahead, wondering where it has all gone, and who persuaded it to go on that paltry morning in December that we now both are remembering so well. Is it not just as if we had never left?

Who is its owner? Who would have taken such liberties to leave it here, this plank in the road? All the cars are stopped, and we are all standing wondering, and even, from time to time, checking our watches. Someone is measuring now, some sensible man from the hardware store. He knows the provenance for sure. He may even have supplied the timber, though not directly. He is a discreet man after all, and we do respect him for that, though respect does not extend to love or mutual bonding, you must understand. The man from the hardware store is always just that, never more than that. And then, without even being asked, he goes to lift the timber because he is a big man with an ingrained attitude of self-promotion. We all encourage him to desist, hold back. After all, it might just be there for a purpose, to prevent something happening, for example, or to point the way somewhere relatively important. Accidents such as this one can be so purposeful. One of us steps up then, kneels down beside it, and looks. No note. No message of any kind, merely a solitary plank of the kind you might use for a floor or even a roof, relatively nondescript. Except that it is here, and nowhere else, and we need to know why, so that the traffic can begin to flow again by and by, and we can all resume our normal lives. On this point we are all agreed. On the other hand, nothing is going to happen soon because there is far too much to be considered, and it stands to reason that we have barely begun. And then, when we have finally got it all done and dusted, it will surely be a matter of calling in the experts. So someone, perhaps in order to ease the rampant pain of all this incertitude, talks of a fire, a barbecue even. Such distractions are good. We surely need to make preparations for the long evening ahead, and so on and so forth.

Being a far-seeing man, my dearest wish was to look into her eye, in order to know far far more than I knew because I had always felt that I knew too little. In times past, when I had approached her in order to ask, she had turned away from me and closed both of her eyes, quite deliberately, in order that I should not see that which there was to be seen, evidently. I asked her then what fears she might be harbouring about me. Was I not quiet and even tempered, small too, and quite tentative in my approaches? What harm could I possibly wish to do her when I had declared such love for her? Others too, many others before, she told me, had asked to look deep into her eyes, and she had always resisted for the obvious reason: being men, they were simply not to be trusted. I stripped down then to my shivering nakedness, in order to prove to her once and for all how harmless I was, how little threat to her was my meagre physique. Take out your eyes, she asked me, in order that I can examine for myself how far they are likely to see. I unscrewed them then, without hesitation. I handed them over. I waited in a mood of the utmost sanctification. I know that in the fullness of recorded time she will return them to me. That is the measure of my love for her. That is the extent to which I trust her, oh foolish, heart-sick man that I am.

She weighed it all in the balance, my entirety, my all. I had waited so long in line, and now it was my turn to be dealt with, my turn to be at the head of the queue, and to feel the press of all that collective envy of those many who were seething at my back. I stood up onto the scales with bated breath, and waited. I tried not to look at the swing of the pointer as it inched up the dial. An unconscionable length of time, that's how I would talk of it now, those minutes I stood there waiting for her verdict. Eventually she said it: fewer than I might have hoped, she remarked, as if to the wall just behind her. Yes, it was that off-hand, that uncaring. How many then? I said, fingering my wallet. Too little even to pay, she said. You are exempt today. You can go on your way with a clouded conscience, young master. I looked at her in disbelief, and then I looked down at myself. I was hoping to observe, with no small measure of pride, how the shirt rounded out my swelling belly, how my thighs thickened out the trousers so that I looked a little like a massy column of the kind you might have seen fallen on its back in the wake of the destruction of a classical temple on the farthest edge of the Syrian desert. Nothing of the kind. Nothing but meagreness in all directions. There was nothing to be done about it, of course. Those massive scales onto which I had stepped, as if mounting the seat of judgment, told the whole of the truth, surely. No machine lies, that much is evident. How could I leave though? Could I not pretend to pay a little something? May I offer a small sum on credit? I asked her. She gave me such a look of contempt that I raised my coat collar and hurried away, hearing nothing of their vituperative comments as I passed on by.

We needed to see for ourselves that the house had not gone forever, even though we knew full well – how could we *not* know? – that the house had gone forever. No house leaves quite that abruptly, at the thunder clap of violent hands, surely? Every house lingers on in memory, for days, years, more than a single lifetime. Every house gets passed on, with great care and attention, and down to the smallest and most cherished of details, to the next generation, who are so eager to listen and to care, and to harbour memories of their own, patched and prinked and composed from your memories, our memories. And so when we arrived at the edge of all that blasted ground, we knelt in pride and shame – yes, it was a little of both – and did our best to conjure it back, creating it again, level brick by level brick, with slivers of grey mortar between, and even setting back in its place (just beyond the courtyard, with its well) beyond the lemon grove, where we used to wander, and the laughter too, ragged, airborne strings of it, that accompanied all our silly talk. Yes, we used to talk like that back then, quite carelessly, just letting go, as if it did not really matter to ourselves or to anyone else what we said or why we had said it. So little was of real consequence when you lived lives quite as idle as ours. And so little mattered now for that matter. That was a lesson to be learned. That was a matter demanding hard thinking.

The piano stood around. It always stood around, loved only a little, and always unplayed. There had been sheet music once, which had filled the wide open mouth of the crude and heavy wooden hod – is that how I might describe it? It always looked a little odd, a little gimcrack to my eye – tucked in underneath, behind the foot pedal, so that you had to get off the stool and feel around, or even crawl towards, and then eventually pull it out. My, what a weight it always was, and always so tight-packed and out-spilling too! Who had ever played all that yellowing music? That was the point, no one ever played it, at least not those days. And no one even remembered when it had last been played – or last been tuned. Perhaps I'm wrong about that. Perhaps I do remember that happening once, when the lid got lifted, and the keys pressed. Quite softly. Quite tentatively. Was that because the tuner was blind? Could that account for such caution? I remember now how the notes sounded jangly and eerie and almost tunelessly otherwise, as if it had lost touch with itself, as if it would never know how to step up and perform any more, even if it were tuned to perfection. And I don't believe that it was ever again tuned to perfection.

I myself came about for no particular reason. No one had asked. No one had ventured even the most casual of enquiries. No one had willed me here, into this house, on this square. I had fallen into it all, as one bundles wooden bricks back into a toybox, bricks that have been strewn around and about the floor. That's what I may once have been, I do believe, idling bits of this and that, nothing deserving of much serious regard. Is that why heads never turned when I entered a room? Is that why I always chose to sit apart, preferring to all human company the sly, playful shift of flames about the coals in the hearth, the way they always danced and wavered, almost as if to entertain me? Yes, they were a great source of entertainment to me then, when I was a child, and they even remain so now, in memory, the way they played their little games of dodge and weave and feint and snuff out, and then, hey presto, only to return again in a thin, bendy flickering of yellow light! How I loved those flames. There was the odd one who would come by and smoke beside me, sharing his fuggy cigarette breath with me, blowing it fiercely out directly ahead so that the flames, startled by such an unanticipated assault, seemed to rear back in either horror or consternation, perhaps a little of both. Did I mind?

Did I even pay them any attention? Not at all. They were both beside me, slotted into the space at random (or so it seemed to me), and not beside me. They were no more remarkable than the wallpaper, and perhaps even a little less lovely because they lacked any sense of rhythm or patterning. Like me, remember, they had just been thrown down in an untidy heap. How can a single world fill itself to the brim with such abundant sources of displeasure?

Dearest sister, begin again. Pick yourself up from the floor and take as a given that the life you have lived so far is not worth more than a single moment's serious attention. I cannot hold myself responsible for you. There is too great a distance between us. I had even forgotten your name. Or almost. I do try my best. And it keeps on returning. In spite of my best efforts. When I chose that name for you, I knew that I was storing up trouble for myself. I would not have chosen to have a sister at all had it not been forced upon me. And it *was* forced upon me with a single condition attached: that I give you a name. I saw no way of avoiding such responsibilities. The pressures of the world bore down upon me, mercilessly. I knew that I had to will you into being. Is this because I needed you? Or did our mother need you? Was a single one, me, not enough for her? Did she relish the upcoming spectacle of one pitted against another, like two wrestlers tight-clenched and sweating in a ring? It was not to be. We remained aloof from each other. Separate rooms. Separate conversations. Separate walks to the same school. Different classrooms. Different opinions. Different friends. Absolute indifference. And now you are in the grip of an overwhelming sadness, and you expect me to pity you, to notice you, to take your part, to comfort you, to tuck you in, to feed you, to advise you, to mollycoddle you, to rock you in a cradle of my own fashioning. You have another think coming. In stripping you of your name – see! I have done it! – I have stripped you of your nature. Let my mother suffer the ignominy of it all. Let her do the donkey work for a change.

The ball must remain in the air. That is the only rule. Everything else is a frivolity – life, time, food, the judiciary. At all times in the air. Pay no respect to night or day. The lights around the perimeter fence will remain undimmed, always. They burn on. And on. And you – all of you – remain inside, eyes on the ball, forever. Pay no heed to those who call it difficult. Life is difficult. Death is less difficult because it is a falling away, a letting go. And this task of ours, this task which bonds us, is supremely difficult because it demands a superabundance of active life at all times. Tension! Action! Concentration! Enthusiasm! Yes, above all things else, an overwhelming enthusiasm for the ball and how it shifts about moment by moment, as it is pushed and thrown and parried and flung. Never once touching the ground. That is the key: never once touching the ground. Is all this impossible? Is life itself impossible? Were you planted down here with tender hands for a given purpose? Well then! This *is* that purpose. Go to!

Life is somewhere between easy and difficult. Sometimes it all depends upon the weather. Good weather can lend such buoyancy to the step. Bad weather drags you down, points back with a sigh to the unmade bed. Sometimes life is easy and difficult simultaneously. You simply do not know where you are in the world. Appearances flash by, some seductive, others repulsive. You snatch out. You miss. You try again. Meanwhile, you are seated at a desk, doing doodles beneath the intense, interrogatory light of a lamp. It's too much. You don't want it. You swallow something and go, at a run, until you stumble, and then quickly die, a matter of months or days or years and years later, when your time has come, the time of the final reckoning up. What did you make of it all? Did you jostle and grumble? Did you fly high? Did you make a spectacle of yourself? Why not ask your favourite authors? They could tell you. They were wise in their time. Perhaps not though. Perhaps it was merely the words that were wise, the words they kept letting go, the words that ran away from them, pell-mell, screaming and crying and pointing back, as they looked on in consternation and near-disbelief. Authors are much like ourselves, feeling their way ahead, with nothing but the ability to set it down, like a dead weight, so memorably though, how bad it all was back then, and how they barely survived it: the unmade bed, that intense, interrogatory light, all the looking out and the wondering.

She kept on saying it and then saying it again. I did not want to hear. I disbelieved every word of it. I did not want the sound of her voice saying it. I wanted something else altogether. Perhaps a dog on a leash, dragging me out to the fields, so that just the two of us could gape and gape at nothing at all. We would lie down together, the dog and I. She would bring out her bone to show me, first carefully unwrapping it from the thin white table napkin, pulling at it so carefully with her teeth. It was such a beautiful bone, with such marrow to be sucked out. Given that she was due to settle into long hours of contentment, I coaxed her up-wood, gently climbing to the picnic table, where a man can hide away from all the world's roughness with a picnic basket and a clean glass and a bottle or two. As it happens, in my mind I had brought such things along with me that day. She lay down at my feet, and settled the bone between her paws, just nudging it at first, as if it were a favourite plaything to be teased. I loved seeing her do that. I especially loved seeing her stretched out on the grass after the third or fourth glass, by which time everything else in life has begun to fall way, rolling down hill to the poppy fields, which are lying fallow until next year. I knew that there was little but barrenness in those fields just now, but I warmed to a little barrenness all the same, silence and barrenness, without the interruption of human voices. Without the interruption of one particular human voice, the one which had stayed with me.

She sits apart from the rest of us in order to count. That is all she ever needs or wants to do. It is her pastime, her life, her undying fervour. She needs an entire table to herself, the largest table in the kitchen, because you never quite know how elaborate the counting will prove to be, what apparatus she may need by way of technical assistance.

We give her everything that she craves, needless to say, we would not wish to be found wanting, we would not want her to strike back at us and make our lives even more miserable than they already are. We want her, daily, hourly, to be serene and occupied amongst us, without rancour, without fears, without the hysterical gushing of tears. I am her father. That much must be clear to to you already. I am responsible for all that she is. It is my burden and my sorrow. Some days I may wish her to be everything that she is not – a young and beautiful girl, for example, who fleets light-footed about the world, turning every eye – but she is not that, and never will she be. And so I would say – let me say it out loud now, in this public forum, in order to test this statement on the air – that I am contented to have contained her here, within the confines of this kitchen, at rest from torment, scrabbling at her workings with her finger ends, muttering her ceaseless calculations out loud from time to time and even, every now and again, leaping up from the table and clapping her hands and weeping for the sheer joy of living.

Albert is not a shadow of himself. He is surely not the no-thing who happens to leave his house from time to time in order to sit on a wall, and take several rounds of deep breathing, and see and hear almost nothing at all, and almost in the world's defiance. He is not that man. He is a much more youthful version of himself, one that I knew well, and would have wished to continue to know. I know so little of this new Albert, although he does resemble overmuch that Albert of old, the one that I loved and will always love, let me make that clear now. I have even sat beside him, on that wall outside his house, close enough to smell the unwashed smell of him, close enough to be repelled by the extent to which he chooses to neglect himself. It is all too repulsive for words, and he knows it. That is why his tight-lipped mouth is set at such an angle of anger and defiance. That is why his entire body seems to quiver when he feels me there, though he does not acknowledge me, ever. I am beyond all acknowledgment. As is he. We are wholly beyond each other. And it is for this reason that I cherish all the more those moments when we would sit together as children, doing barely anything at all, spinning a marble, a colour-striated marble, on its axis, and staring together – as if nothing else really mattered, then or whenever – as it slowed to a stop, and then settled, in that dip in the asphalt just beyond the back door.

You see, it had been a door once. I had seen it here, in this very space where I am now standing, helplessly looking about, feeling my way these days. What else is there for me now? What else am I to be invited to attach myself to? It had all the pridefulness, all the indomitability of a solid door, all the composure, the heft, the assurance, the fight-back, that a door seems to demand of itself, that ability to exclude the world, to say no when no is demanded of it, to be an impassioned moralist, he who decides whether to admit or not to admit. As simple as that. And so, quite tentatively at first, I found myself leaning against it again, just as I might once have done, that old black, weathered door, the house door through which we always passed. There was only ever this door, this single door, this singular door. The back door was not a door at all. It was for servants, thieves, sneaks, nobodies, those who, once indoors, had to pretend that they were not in fact there at all because their presence amongst us registered not at all. Nobody knew who they were. They looked through them. Or past them. If they spoke, nobody ever heard or even listened because such speech was not regarded as human speech at all. I push a little harder. It is taking my weight! I am not falling through the air! I am at the door again, on the outside of the door, waiting to be admitted, waiting my turn, waiting in line, with an infinity of patience. Yes, they are angry when I step up and push against. There are many in front of me now, you see, as there always were, even in the best of times. How long will I be required to wait? Just as long as it always takes? That long? And yet it was always worth it, I do recall, to be admitted in the end, that is what I – that is what we all – lived for. There was no alternative to waiting outside the door. And, even now, when the space looks so blank and so unpromising, there is no alternative to waiting outside the door.

All the men, women and children who meant so much to me in my life, I have lined them all up opposite me here, in this courtyard, where the sun beats down remorselessly until sunset. In spite of the general goodwill I feel towards them, I may no longer have the strength to meet and to greet them all because there are so many of them here, and they are all so ready to tell me their stories, I see that by the eagerness with which they each catch my eye when I turn to one or another of them, wave (rather shyly because some of them I scarcely recognise at all), and give a little smile. They all know me! There is no doubt whatsoever that I meant so much to them at different moments of our lives – or perhaps of their lives. And yet it still shocks me. How could it be – I am marvelling at it all now – that I have touched upon the lives of all these people, and in so many different places? I do not even recall having visited such a variety of locations. Some of them are not on the mainland at all! And would I even have known such people? My type of person is so small and so set apart from all the rest, reluctant to speak, reluctant to give too much, lest the little that is there to be given gets spilled, needlessly. I have always kept myself tight pressed close to myself. That has always been my recipe for survival. And in spite of that, there are all these people here, and they have been gathered together by no one but myself, and they all claim to have known me! And now I am faced with the unenviable task of speaking to them all, of asking them how and when and from where they all know me, and what I meant to them, and whether I had a benign influence upon their lives. Or not. Or not! Yes, there is always the possibility that they will tell me that I utterly disgusted them, that I was an abomination in their lives, and that they had only returned here to tell me all about the worst of myself. I feel inclined to disperse them by calling on the help of an almighty plague wind. A voice tells me to hesitate.

I always find a use for prayer. Prayer will always have its moments. It is akin, I feel, to the creation of a sacred building which rises and rises, as if by some miracle, in front of you, word by small word, each one a building block, a citadel of sorts in the making, which then comes to loom, quite magnificently, over you. That is the paradox, you see, that is the miracle of it all, your words are so small, and often uttered inwardly, hushed as a whisper, so that no one could ever hear, even were another human head to be pressed so breathing close next to yours. They are so small, I say, those words of yours, and yet the fruits of all that fervent whispering are something mighty and tall, something which looms and overawes and causes you to fall to the ground in wonderment. Did your merest words, those humble things, bring about such a marvellous outcome? Are you even capable of such a thing? And yes, yes yes, that building tells you, by its very presence in front of you, you have done it, you have summoned up all that he means to you, this deity who has so long seemed to elude you, to prayers quite as fervent as your own, he will listen. He will heed and reward. He will demonstrate to you what power he wields in your life when you show your great love for him, and how he will never abandon you.

<hr />

Is this enough? she said to him one evening as they were leaving the office together. He had been careful to turn off all the lights. There was such a need to be careful these days, to waste nothing. He looked at her then, he turned back to see her following him, and she was dangling it from her hand, that single puce glove. How am I to know? he replied. How am I to know what your body needs? They both knew that winter was upon them, and how fiercely it bit. Would a single glove do? But why not two gloves? Why not *two*? Could a single glove ever really suffice? Then he remembered all about her tragedy, and he felt ashamed. He remembered all the pain she had suffered, how she had howled and screamed so terribly that everyone had heard her, across the whole extent of the factory floor and even up into his office, a tragedy which meant that she would only ever need a single glove until the end of her days, she who had once worn both gloves – like everyone else. And so he said what he knew that he needed to say. The question is, he replied, pointing down at it as it dangled from her hand, how thick it needs to be, and that requires us to know the imponderable: how the weather is faring beyond the door... They both nodded. They both understood, of course. The offices were so unnaturally hot, always, so hot that you had to strip down to your shirt sleeves! All inside spaces were hot in this country – from civic buildings such as this one to the apartment blocks where they all lived, everything was always so overheated that even in the winter months, there were times when you had to fling the window wide to admit a little coldness. Oh the relief of coldness after all that fug! He flung wide the street door then. The snow blew back into their faces. She nestled at his back. He felt how she shivered. Oh my, he muttered, oh my dear God above, what a world this is in which we do live!

He never quite knew whether there was enough of it, whether or not he needed more. Thickening it out, giving it shapeliness of some kind, that was always a problem. Causing it to stand on its own two feet, observe how it walked – or keeled over. So much keels over. So much barely has a chance. Too hopeless. Too helpless. Too fragile. Why begin at all in that case? But was not that why we were here at all, to begin and then to carry on, willy nilly, unquestioning, to a degree at least? He was not talking about anything in particular, you must understand. He was standing, bony bare legs still pressed against the side of the bed, one arm part thrust into his shirt sleeve, a single sock idly dangling like some airborne worm from his left foot. He was idly musing, you could say. He was wondering to himself how worlds come into being, any worlds, worlds of any description, worlds of human invention, worlds of god's invention. Each one does his bit, plays his part. It is as if nothing seems to matter at first, when you are young and without a care in the world. Something pushes you forward, a gentle wind of sorts, a kind of mild-mannered forward propulsion, and you find yourself going along with it because there is nothing else to be done. You would not be aware of any alternative anyway. You are far too inexperienced for that sort of thing. Then the door bangs open and you find yourself distracted, if not mildly irritated, being, as ever, part naked and part clothed. Being flustered, now that's something else altogether.

If you think that this is goodbye, in part you would be right. It is not of my own choosing, you must understand. You brought me here, and then you said: now is your moment. Excuse me, I replied, it is not my moment. If it's anyone's moment, it is yours. You scoffed at me then. You let your mouth hang open. You scratched at your arm pit because that's what apes always do when the fleas get too maddening. I turned away. I concentrated on the beauty of the countryside where I was still walking, the apparent smoothness of the hills, and how the clouds hang over them. I always go for a short, fast-paced walk in the out-of-doors when things begin to gnaw at me somewhat. I'm sure you'd agree.

The entire land lies still now, stretching away, as if yawning to itself. Nothing stirs. Nothing has any particular wish to make itself known. There is a general idleness hanging over it all, some sense that everything has been done once and for all, that exertion would prove to be ridiculous in the end. Whose wish was that one? Not mine, certainly. There is now an end to all wishes. I too have melded and merged, a lump of clay which lies me down beside another, the two indistinguishable from each other. How is it that you came walking just then, as if all was to be re-made, as if the end of thought, that very idea of the end of all thinking, had been erased at a stroke? Did you do it? It must have been you. There was no one else. Everything else is at peace in this world of terminal blankness. Frankly, your running hither and thither does disturb me. There is no need for it any more. The training has ended, that hitherto wish to go far, to see beyond all seeing, all those old yearnings, all these minuscule matters have been long since laid away. You seem to be in defiance of all of this, as if you have never heard – or never heeded when told. I can believe that of you, you prickly little devil of a woman. Your spirit always grated on me. You were always a creature of defiance above all things else. What are you doing just now then? Who gave you that mattock, that rusted mattock? You are digging and delving again – see how your sweat is pouring! Such enthusiasm for turning the clod that is me! You may live to regret it. Yours is a contrary way of being.

And, speaking for myself, I simply could not countenance yet another journey.

The two stones lived quite harmoniously, each one ignorant of the other, because they were separated by such enormous distances. Had they been a little closer, had some embodiment of sheer malevolence thought to shift one or another of them – it scarcely matters which for the sake of this argument – across plain, down valley, and even over seas, things might have been a little different. Each could have got wind of the other's thinking. Each one could have thought this of the other: speaking for myself alone, that is not quite how I would choose to think. There would have emerged, little by little, a general unease, some growing belief that someone was wrong somewhere, that there were matters not only to be discussed, but also contested; that, in short, all was not quite as smoothly shaped and prinked and patterned as it had always seemed to be. And then what would have happened? Well, there would have been wars, perhaps low-level skirmishes at first, and then, almost inevitably, a general conflagration. The world as we know it would have been turned on its head. It would have become unrecognisable to itself. All carefully contrived systems of jurisprudence, for example, would have been burnt on the general pyre in an exciting upwards swirl of smoking, flame-licked paper, and we would all have found ourselves oafishly standing around, beer guts to the fore, cheering it on, as if madness were the solution to all things... Which it may not be, of course.

I twist and I turn in this chair for a very specific reason, you must understand. There is this chilling distinctness to be recognised. We do not share a common language – in spite of every argument to the contrary. We do not even share a common face. That would be impossible. Why bother even to raise the matter? Is this after all nothing but a box of tomfooleries? Your chair is attached, unbudgeable, unshiftable, to the floor, facing out to the mountains and the lake, for a very good reason. The same mountains. The same lake. Call it a gesture of reassurance. I have no wish to see you. It would not be wise even for us to acknowledge each other. No good would come of it. Too much poison would gush into a common drain. That is why we face in opposite directions. I stare down at the little pool, with the weaving toy carp, the windmill and the trees, so bare and so wintry on this late April morning. It is more than enough for me. What is more, were things to be otherwise arranged, the same old problem would rear up again: whether or not we knew each other when we both strutted about the garden, lopping flower heads as if neither of us had a care in the world. I have no wish to know the answer to that question. I have no wish to facilitate your posing it again. Hence the mouth tape. Hence the pot of glue.

Numbers are all our goodness. If we wish – and we *do* wish from time to time – we can climb them, two by two, as one might even climb a ladder, with such youthful, airborne ease, and peer out from there towards those promised lands of plenty: my land, all our lands... Or we can squat betwixt and between and speak to one or another, or pair them together in order to tune in to gently overheard conversations. What did 103 have to say to 74 today? Was it fruitful? Did they experience an exquisite degree of mutual gratification? Of course they did! Why though? Because such exchanges have been robbed of all potential friction, all the potential awkwardness of human interchange. It is all so clean, how they speak. Nothing casts a shadow. There is no sidereal rumble, no shadow of resentment or suspicion soon to be hanging over. Numbers are our model of perfection, aren't they?

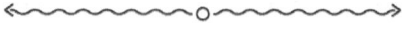

The relief, at the last, as our final gestures of bewilderment faded from view, was almost overwhelming. We congratulated each other. To have travelled such distances unharmed! To have prevaricated as we did – and yet still to have come through! There was a space for new things at last – and even a mutual acknowledgment of sorts that the old things still mattered, the dear old things, of such fragile, faltering memory. Your chair, for example! Or the way that the fish tank in the bedroom, after so many years of quiet self-reflection, began, almost unnoticed at first, to leak a little and even to bubbly-murmur... We took it all in such good stead – as we take it in good stead now, knowing all that we have been, spread out as it all is like a field of gold across his plain. The fumbles and the stumbles, the nasty, sharp wounds of love, none of it seems to matter any more. The train is moving with such ease through cuttings – such thrilling occlusions! – beside the blindingly delightful fields of rape, our fields after all, no one else's! How fortunate we now are. How could we have misunderstood it all for so long, believing ourselves to be beneath that enduring curse! What simpletons we were! What dullards! Now we are free to speak it all out loud as water gushes from a spring in the mountains, yes all these words of ours come together, a terrible, wondrous cacophony of words, and each one beloved by the one who did the uttering. Did you say that you were now inclined to sleep for a while, that the past days and years have all been a little too much for you, given your fragile temperament? So be it! Sleep on! What you have achieved already is towering above you! There will be none like you again. Take pleasure in your own complacency. I do. And I am little more than the shredded rag of a fitful companion.

<~~~~~o~~~~~>

It was always an overlong conversation. From time to time we paused to take a nap. The lights blazed on. The office lights never failed. Light followed dark out into the world beyond, the world beyond the drawn blinds, that world we saw so seldom in the Conference Season. The ashtrays were emptied regularly, and no one admired the shabby greyness of our suits more than me. There were seventeen of us around each table, each circular table, and eye met eye, burningly, without flinching. Was there ever a pause for the rapid mastication of food, the swift gulping down of water, coffee, tea? Perhaps. Perhaps not. Such matters were not to the point. It was our being there which counted. We were the very pillars of the building in which we sat, and without our sitting there, all would have thinned away into nothingness. It was the boomings and the counter-boomings of our mightily assured voices which counted, at which we all froze in fear, knowing exactly how much we feared each other in this our great Conference Season! And what exactly was determined on these occasions? Nothing that I now recall. I recall most of all how it ground on and on, pitilessly, and with the utmost solemnity, and oh how, when we left again after weeks and months, as shabby, grey and sweat-stained as our suits, we knew that we had done our duty, and that the word DUTY was written across the very sky across which our fighter jets zoomed as we saluted them, heels clicking.

The beauty of Miranda is written down, described with minute particularity, in this notebook of mine. I saw her just the once, and that was more than enough for me. No one has remained more vividly alive to me throughout my entire life. Do I ever regret not having known or seen her again? Do I not regret that on that single occasion, when I saw her light-skipping across a traffic-choked road, that the noise of the passing, circumambient world was so great that, even had she opened her mouth to speak to her older female companion – she herself was little more than a child – I would have had no chance at all of hearing her voice? And so my Miranda has always been a silent Miranda. What is more, my view of her as she crossed that road, at a run and a skip, was often obscured by lorries, cars, bicycles, and so the portrait I hold of her still in my mind's eye is fitful, patchy and discontinuous. Has this much mattered? Not at all! If anything, it has made my cloistered life up here in the deep shadows of the Tuscan hills a little simpler. Unlike myself, she has never aged or weathered. When I am inclined to feel somnolent or remorseful or doleful, I have conjured her in such a way that she has always been a steady consolation to me. When I have felt loveless and strangely absent, she has laid her hand across my forearm – even as I have been committing words or marks to paper – yes I both draw her and write of her – and reassured me of her love for me. It is all I might ever have wished for.

Can you make something of it? I have made something of it. Can you reassure yourself that it will continue? It has long continued. It will continue to continue. Can it be carried for the required distances? It is portable. I fashioned it so that it would be portable – and disposable too – if and when the hour demanded such an outcome. Are you satisfied with things as they are then? There is no alternative to things as they are. I have closed the door, firmly, on my decision-making. Nor would I describe your enquiries as impertinent because I am beyond all that fiddle-faddle.

She described it to me, with no small contempt, as a makeshift way of doing things. She was speaking to me from deep within her laboratory, of course, with her pie charts and her unfathomably mystical calculations. I was out here in the road, amongst the very worst that any day might be inclined to throw at me, thumbing a lift to somewhere upon whose fixed identity I was yet to batten down. And that is how it will always be, I said, speaking to myself in a level, measured fashion, and with the customary assurance. That is how I am to be planned, shaped, nurtured, in so far as I am planning, shaping and nurturing myself at all. Yes, all feels good in this world to a blind man such as myself. It is so good to feel and not to see, more thrillingly unpredictable. A presumed head metamorphoses into a gourd, the sensuality of a tight squeezed sponge is unknowable to he who looks and then passes on with a yawn. What is more, I am my own best guarded secret. My eye sockets are milky blanks – no clue there then. I never grasp hold of another's hand with any meaning because no meaning can be anticipated by a blind man. It is all seek and find, seek and find. I begin again without prior knowledge, having wiped myself clean of the excitement of anticipation. It is good that this should be so because there is no abyss to be contemplated. Merely this perpetual, gentle wafting hither and thither as I sit here and do nothing at all to be seen by the world with all its voracious appetite...

He was there painfully early, asking the usual difficult questions. I pointed to the wood pile and the tools. He knew them well enough. He had left them strewn there as a way of making a point, of that I had no doubt. I had spent the intervening weeks and months stepping over them, and once even leaping for the sheer dare of it. Needless to say, nothing had been disturbed. I busied myself elsewhere as he prowled around the perimeter, the usual growl of discontent in his throat. I do not know why he puts himself through it. I had not asked him to do this work. He had been a volunteer like all the rest, for god's sake, and an eager one to boot. Even his hair was standing on end that morning! There had been words, a few, and perhaps some instructions (even fewer of those because, frankly, I did not much care in which direction it faced. The notion of feng shui is not in my vocabulary.) And now he creeps up here once in a while with such a burden of misery about him that I find myself even pitying his state. Who is to blame though? I do not need it. I have outhouses in plenty. He could have built it elsewhere. He could have remained in his own country. He need not have had anything to do with this impossible terrain, with its fiercely upjutting rocks and its unpredictable mud slides.

I have never known how love tolls, and indeed whether it ever tolls at all. I have listened and listened. Silence has engulfed me, the silence of the absence of a credible answer to my ceaseless, hopeless quest. Is there really love in the tolling of a bell? I have asked myself over and over. And then I have listened to church bells in order to say to myself, perhaps by way of reassurance: this is love scattering itself across the graveyards, and then far into the fields. Others come looking and listening too – women, men, stray dogs. They stand around and sniff the air, as if behaving with meaning and purpose. They pretend to disturb the ground with a toe, or to peer deep into a municipal waste bin as if something important has been mislaid, something which they cannot stop themselves seeking. It is all about love, I hazard, I guess. I think I know that by the way that they do not look outwardly when they look. Their quest is entirely inward. I can see that by the way in which their gaze never seems to leave the eye of the gazer. They even blunder into each other – I have seen a man being bundled into a ditch, and then drag himself out, mud-soaked – and then quickly apologise. It is always such a private, such a personal quest. The problem is that no one really knows the sound of love. The bell's note may be the gravest of errors. It may be pushing us far away from love, to the uttermost limit of lovelessness. It may be a trick on the part of some embodiment of sheer malevolence. Who knows? Who can ever know?

There was one letter still to be answered or dealt with, and if I left myself the breathing space of a day or two longer, I knew in my heart of hearts that I would find the courage within myself to unseal the envelope. At least, I sincerely hoped that this might be the case. Meanwhile, it sat there on the windowsill, sun-warmed when the sun shone out, within sight of the harbour and the lifeboat and the eager running children. How they loved to run and to run, those children! And how often in those days did we hear the lifeboat's siren, at all hours of the day and night, calling the volunteers out, and then into the dangers of the sea. I often used to think to myself as I lay awake thinking of them running towards the boat, even as they pulled on their protective clothing and their boots, how much akin that call was to the call of this letter of mine, which had lain here on this window sill for so many years now, waiting for me to lose my fear of it, waiting for me to rise to its challenge.

We are all gathered here again on this grey morning in June, watching the tall ships leaving once again from the harbour. How many times will they go on leaving and leaving in this way? How many days will we be required to turn up with our handkerchiefs and our suitcases and our tears? Look now! See how soundlessly they move through the mist, and out into these churning, voracious waters. It is as if they scarcely exist at all. It is as if I am writing them into existence even as I am describing their departure to you. I think myself onto the foredeck of the one which leads all the rest out into the sound. I am at the prow again, looking out, and listening to none of the cries at my back, none of the cries overhead, paying attention to nothing other than the sound of my own regular breathing. Yes, it is regular and steady and calm this morning in spite of the tumult of the sea, in spite of how we turn and rise and lean and weave. Why did so few of us choose to board this ship that will lead us so proudly out and beyond? Did the rest of them fear the consequences of their actions? I at least was ready for it all. The pack of cards is in my pocket, and the compass is strapped to the red bandanna that encircles my brow. And now there remains only the small matter of writing it all down, of possessing the wherewithal to reach out to one and all, because there is so much to be said, always, by a tongue-tied man such as myself. Yes, I shall be ready for that because without my words washing back and forth, back and forth remorselessly, you will surely be rudderless again, and I would not wish that fate to befall even the worst of my enemies, of whom there are evidently many, I do see.

Yes, I entered the room after him, after he had agreed not to speak. We had both taken that same vow of silence in order to transform ourselves from those pagans of old, to fine, upstanding religious people of the present and coming moments, with piety as our end view. This is why he walks and talks so cautiously, as if the entire world deserves an apology. He is meek, humble and small, and soon enough, with due self-chastisement, I shall be like him. We will both walk, small and sorrowful, side by side in this world of sorrows. And everyone will know us for who and what we are. We will be their exemplars, the light which shines steadily down upon them, illuminating the darkest of their dark corners, relentlessly. Pioneering of this kind is what appeals to us. We have spent too long regretting the mis-steps of the past.

As he walked out of the door in front of me, I tried to muster words sufficient unto this august occasion, but they would not come. It was my only opportunity, I was aware of that. I knew that I would never be so close to him again, that he would melt back graveward – as if he were some phantasm – after he had passed through the street door of the surgery. As I watched him there, a little stooped over with the practical difficulty of it all, I simply could not believe that this man who was not-so-gently manipulating the knob of the door in a mood of rising exasperation, that this man could really be the one who had made it all so difficult for us ever after. Part of me wanted to shout him down for his superiority, to tell him to his face that four hundred years or so means nothing at all – that it is akin to a wisp of straw in the wind. The fact is that it was all still with us, everything that he had done, everything that he had written, and we did not really want it to be there because it meant that all we writers who came after had proceeded with bent backs, helplessly, hopelessly dragging our feet as we went, staring ahead at the nothingness of our futures. He had turned us into little better than lisping children, this man. We simply were unable even to exist as ourselves. He had single-handedly stripped us of all confidence, all courage. Given that Shakespeare was still having some difficulty with the knob of the door, I tweaked at his doublet and said: may I do it for you? Not a word did he say. There was fear and furtiveness in his look as he watched me turn the knob and release him back into the past.

Take it back then, take it all back. Or as much as you please. It means nothing to me. I cannot make your words rise at all. They lie flat on the bottom of the mixing bowl like unkneaded dough. I would that everything were different today, but it is not. Nothing is different. I woke up with the same head ache and the same call, so pitiful, from the door. I got up. I pulled on my boots. It was raining out there, a mean and slanting downpour. I waited a while. It was still raining. I tried a word or two in order to get things going. *Hosanna in the Highest.* Did that make a blind bit of difference? No it did not. I may be my own worst enemy. I wish you good night then. Could you ever feel your way towards a modicum of charity? There are only so many questions to be asked.

Part Two

God's Heaven

Then we entered that strange country again, known to no more than two or three. How do you know? you asked me. I was there, I replied. I did the counting. I also provided everything that was needful. You were still slithering along on your back, needless to say. I did not know how to help at first. Now I know that a song – just one – makes the difference between life and death for you. I am so glad that you told me that. It was amongst the two or three things that you have ever told me. Five years is a long time. Does it seem longer to you too?

⇐~~~~~o~~~~~⇒

The metronome was a gift. Open-handed. Of such a near unbearable loveliness too! Teak. And how it gleamed in the lamplight! We used to sit side by side and watch the needle's incessant movement, from one side to the other, as if it were falling into a dreamless sleep and then, all of a sudden, jerking awake again, being mindful of itself in unanticipated ways. Did you love me just then? The power of my concentration was as much as you have ever remarked upon. On this day at least. There were others. Correction: there will always be others. Years maybe of hazarding... Or maybe not. The breeze may just be lifting away. Who can ever know what will get carried off or abandoned?

⇐~~~~~o~~~~~⇒

How the waves parted just then to reveal a bank of shingle on which, having fallen, we rested our bodies... How far had we come though? Was it at dawn that we started? Or yesterday's dawn? Your bland and equable smile wiped all queries away, needless to say. We had the two books with us, the water-resistant books. I had scarcely begun to write mine. Yours had been much longer in the telling. Entirely consistent with your character. I had just the one pen, you had two, etc. It was all such a dance of vanities. How we tolerated it all back then, with so much still to come, I do not know. Perhaps the push of the waves, and the strange and surprising warmth enveloping the toes, had something to do with it. We were such suckers for daylight. Always have been.

⇐~~~~~o~~~~~⇒

The entrypoint took in animals, I ask you. Who has ever kept an animal away when you crave to be on your own, breathing god's good air? They jostled and they snorted and they tried to heave us aside, wrong-foot us. The meanies. Neat and swift butchery was the only answer. I am good at that. You did not know that I was even capable of such deft side-strokes. I had never needed to tell you before, and certainly not in those days of drawing-room pleasantries, with the boasting emerging from mouths alongside such delicate and prolonged (needlessly?) finger movements. Have I exaggerated what you mean – have meant – to me? More to the point, have you?

This is too much of everything. Too many trains. Too much food. Overmuch conversation of a kind that gluts the mind and leaves the stomach feeling sated and churning. I for one would prefer to skip over the fields, gambol like a lamb, chew the cud ever so slowly along with the cows. Would they have us in that field? They are in conclave just now, with their backs to us, tails switching like lashed ropes. Could we ride them? Are they that kind of a beast? Surely not. Nor are we.

I gamble. It's what I do. It defines me from just about every angle: stoop (extreme), brow (furrowed), fingers (flexing and grasping). You look good, almost water-purified, beside me. I really don't understand why you stay here at all when there is always so much space around you primed for immediate occupation. Your look of extreme exasperation suggests that you need to be elsewhere, quickly, if not now. Meanwhile, I go about my hourly, daily business, shovelling the chips, digging ever deeper into the pocket. No one has asked me yet to define paradise. Were that to happen ever, you would find me standing here like any other good old man of a certain vintage, cock-sure poised and ready.

The child is a small and blundering beast that we pretend to love and to cherish. And we do! We do! Why otherwise take the trouble to fashion such a creature? Then there is a matter of language, the blurts and the blabs and the coos. In time there will be much talk to be had of focus, training, exercise of muscles. Until that time, there may be a glimpse of paradise to be savoured in all these hyper-swift movements from crotch to mouth and onward.

Simple. No trickery about it. Measure the days by whatever it is that you take away with you. You tell me you take nothing. I pity you then. I even pity the bench out there in the sun that you sit on. It deserves better. Were I to be sitting there, I would give it an entire lifetime of ribaldry. Come to think of it, I have lived the life of a bench through and through, and more than once. Sometimes it is the night and all its circumambient aloneness that I have found captivating. At other times I have raised my fat lips to the rain. You just choose.

Lack-a-day! she cried, the determined medievalist, as if to encourage us to move backwards. I was in an argument with breakfast just then – as were you, I must point out – and it is for this reason that we did not see her. It was Robin Hood, that rude snatch of campery in top-to-toe green, who brought her – dragged her more like – to us, spilling much obtuse laughter from the side of his mouth. I had never been aware that he had gathered about himself such a boisterous company. You choose something new to discover every day, do you not, even when the possibilities seem grey, grey, grey? I mean, of course: do *I* not? Forgive me for such presumption. After the morning had settled down, the light began to tease in these parts as if it were any other game of naked poker.

Lingering on after the May showers had passed away, we gathered no more than a quorum of true believers to investigate the latest news that had just now fallen with such a bang on the table. One or two picked about gingerly, careful to use finger-ends only, as if sorting through many loose-leaf pages of no-holds-barred unpleasantries. I have no idea why it all became quite so gloomy. You have always known it to be like this, as have we. We agreed to go by the old routines on every second Thursday, and this is undeniably that day. Has the water closet not been playing up again? Do you walk around with your eyes habitually closed when there is always so much still to be done? The Saviour of the World has not yet been a subject of loose, bat-back-and-forth conversation this morning. I have no doubt that we will get around to it when all other topics have fallen away into meaninglessness. Such is the way of things.

There were these woods set down, without explanation or apology. It had not happened before. We had chosen this place on account of the fact that it had been described by the eager and overly youthful vendors to be *an uninterrupted urban environment*, with every opportunity set down and listed, one two three, by way of a collective gift from all the neighbours, of which there were said to be hundreds already. Not at all. We were alone here today (and ergo perhaps every day) with all these trees, trees, trees which possessed such a capacity to whisper at each other non-stop that by the third day after our arrival (having travelled in some style by that neat little paddle boat from the coast), we were standing outside beside the water pump feeling quite unnerved by it all. What could there be to do? Being a sucker – the world's worst – for acquiescence, I slung a hammock between two of the more manageable ones and re-strung the ukelele. At a stroke, the world seemed more amenable. I also took a quiet vow just then to ignore you for a little while. What am I to do if you rip off your clothes and pour paraffin all over everywhere? I would never have called myself a mental health professional. On the other hand, I am likely to come round to you in the end because these trees hold a strictly limited appeal for me.

Days are like two dice flung down at random onto a table top. They roll around, do a fancy little pirouette or two, and then they settle. They always settle. Similarly, days happen in the way that they do. There are no announcements, no one to tell you that this is how it will always be, and you just have to make the best of it. You find yourself, fresh awake, startled back here, and bang slam whop in the middle of it all. Perhaps there will be a chicken noise off to the left if they keep chickens in the next garden. Likely not. There are no gardens. It is a sea of black asphalt in every direction which rucks and rears like a badly fitted carpet when the sun beats down. Why put us here, at this particular angle of view to one another, at this particular angle of view to all this pitiless, stinking, fresh laid asphalt? I feel like a relatively simple mathematical problem waiting to be solved by someone much younger than I have ever been or could ever have hoped to be. Why was I born so old? Will I die sooner or later? I doubt it. There is far too much thinking to be done of this kind. And perhaps of other kinds too. Would I be unkind to myself if I were to tell you that I quite enjoy it?

Well, this is how it happened. I was lifting the lid of the bin, priming myself for a little new, albeit somewhat untidy, syncopation. You must have heard something even before anything really happened! That is what I call the beginning of a relationship which threatens to last. And it has lasted. Even before I could adjust the angle of the stick in my hand in relation to the lid, you had seized hold of it as if it were your right or something. I was furious at first. Who is the drummer in this world? I shouted. You scarcely needed to reply. I had seen your muscles. I had seen the way you shimmied across the yard. In fact, I had already deftly thrown you a pillow. The future must be said to arrive much sooner then.

Is it? Or is it not? I would not describe it as such. If you are fearful, just walk away. There is always plenty of scope to be someone else. There are many examples. You may even have seen one or two of them without quite recognising what you were looking at because your eyes are always so inclined towards the ground. I have it in mind to lift you in the direction of the perpendicular. There is no reason for you to be down there as if someone you never knew had called you a floor, and you had agreed to agree without giving the matter even so much as a moment's thought. I expect better than this from you. I know you for everything that you might yet become. Trust me to guide you gently into our paradisal garden. You will come to understand that even a weed may be as proud as the world itself.

Walk back to the beginning. Is that a little better for you now? Is your seeing equal yet to this lamplight's seeing? Would you – could you ever – claim that much? Let me do it for you then. Easy does it. We could whistle.

In the evenings the general ruckus would begin. And then it would die away again, as if it had never been. It is a matter of being reconciled to whatever happens along, I told you, with some nonchalance, from the chimney corner or the inglenook as you always insisted on calling it, being so pernickety about terms such as these. You were already sleeping, and, truly, I do like the sight of you there, nodding, dreaming your old dreams, breaking back into your inner self like some thief in the night. And so the days passed by. Why would they not? You took up knitting, and, as ever, I acquiesced in your choices. You have it over me, always. I do forgive you for that. I forgive myself too. Who would not if they had an amenable disposition? All roads lead nowhere eventually. That is today's mantra, and I am not yet sick of it. Speak for yourself, lippy lady.

The truck driver leant over to say a word or two. That was the winter the wolves returned in such packs we had to move out for a couple of months, until things settled down somewhat. I have no objection to city life. I just don't want it to last too long. I always thirst after the next best thing. Why did you cry out so consistently, on those nights I was doing my level best to be quiet? There is no counting on your moods. We travel together, that's all there is to be said about it really, hugger mugger as the old phrase goes, the one I do like so much because it just feels so right, especially when the chill descends again. All roads will prove inseparable in the final days. There is no getting away from it. Reality sticks like glue, does it not? I never shake it off. One day I call myself a new man, poignantly so, and then the dull aches return as if they never went away. Who could ever live with such a man? I do, hourly, daily. You reconcile yourself to what goes on. You breathe in and out, steadily. How do I know? Because I am listening. I have your interests at heart.

I like the way you descend the stairs in all your essential nudity. You offer yourself like a gift to me. Except that you do not, not really, because as soon as I turn in your direction, show some genuine, heartfelt interest, you return whence you came, back to the bedroom, and put your coat, gloves and hat back on, the beaver-skin hat that you always wear for inclement weather. I can hear you racing to pull them on just in case I bestir myself. I never do. I am too busy with my reading, which eases, naturally enough, into a morning's hard musings on your behaviour, how I enjoy it so much from time to time before too much indifference again seizes hold of me, and I return (as one surely must) to close-scrutinising the steady tick of the metronome on the kitchen table. Life has always fallen out like this. It is a matter of showing some patience. Who would ever want to live on the outer extremity?

I have nothing but admiration for these hills, the energy and spirit that they have shown in order to rise so high. I also secretly admire the fact that no one and nothing ever tried to stop them. There could have been at least one or two level plains hereabouts, surely, to lodge some serious objections with the relevant authorities. No one ever did. They just let things fall out as they have, and I am quite glad about that, the fact that nature seems to shape herself with such quiet determination. I myself don't have the pluck or the energy to do in my turn whatever it would take, not really. I am a spectator of such things as hills, not a maker of grand structures. Unless I am being forced to speak just a little of myself, of course. You could say that I have played no small part in whatever it is that has been made of myself. I have, yes, made certain choices. I have even colluded somewhat at my own education of sorts – when I was not soundly asleep at my desk beside the window. I have faced down one or two in my time, the one or two who deserved it, the one or two who stuck out like sore thumbs. You know who you are, ladies and gents.

You could say that gratitude is so much pap. Squeeze it and it melts away. That is why I have always described myself as a free spirit. I commune with rocks and crustaceans. They are my milieu. Odd? Who are you to describe me so! Did you not build roads where only Nothingness had reigned supreme for millennia? What gall you have! On the other hand, I could never have done such a thing. I would have hung back, and perhaps even re-considered. In the mornings – listen to this – the table light winks on and off even when it is not wanted, even when the sunlight has begun to needle its way through the blinds. It is then that I get up, with you beside me from time to time.

Next to this – nothing. Nothing at all. Blank spaces. No memories to be shared. I am giving you the truth. I would have no reason to lie to you. Had I known you before, things might have been different, of course. Had we had – as they say – some *common history*. But we don't. I don't even recognise this coat you have flung across the settee. It stinks, you know. You should have washed it before you came. It's the very least you could have done.

Crossways. Crossed swords. Crossed staves – and medievalism! To live in those stirring times, heart always racing, on one's mettle. Or straight up, affirming the perpendicular. Or perhaps declining, on sleepy days, to the horizontal. It is the horizontal which most appeals to me. At floor level. The long contemplation of the skirting board and the mouse hole, just one, or perhaps even two if they are lucky. Yes, in times such as these, to be low-lying, and saying almost nothing. The only movement, inward, that of the imagination, conjuring entire worlds of recklessness while saying nothing, flickering not even so much as an eye lash.

Could you please just wait for a moment or two before you speak? Too much has been suggested already. Entire cities have been planned, and even submitted in embryonic form. We are not quite ready for such extreme venturesomeness. We would ask you to step back for a day or two, to slip your shoes back on as quietly and as meekly as possible, and to return whence you came. We don't even recognise the language. That has to be the first impediment. Take this textbook. Study the mutterings of real men before you approach us again, in all meekness, in all humility, some years from now, when the days are clement, and the sap again rising.

The cats rose up as one, all of them, pleading for a little consideration. I mean those tiresome *men* in catsuits of course, the jokers who deal in alternative religions – baubles, feathers, and book-length fantasies of the kind we habitually relish. It was a matter of appeasement, with much dancing at first, slow turns to the left and then to the right, at the advice of the noonday sun and other supernumeraries. All seemed to go well enough until the rain and the thunder emphatically spoke otherwise. I can understand that well enough. There is always a time to speak and a time to remain silent. My ancestors excelled themselves on the monocycle. No one has ever tried to deny that the ancient Assyrians were the go-to people for lion-hunting.

In the cleft of this stick, that is where the truth is said to lie, the unvarnished truth. Begin again perhaps, on any Saturday morning in June, when nothing has fallen out as you might have anticipated that it would. Secretly, all this has rather pleased you. Is that not a fact? What is more, there were crinolines in the wardrobe when you called to look, as if you might have been visiting some shop of ancient memory, of the kind that your own grandmother would surely have frequented just before her wedding day. Ah yes, the ease of it all, when it slows down to walking pace, 'dreaming pace' I might even have said, had you given me the nod, tipped me the wink. Or even spoken more crisply. At least we are agreed on that! Let us remember her now. Let us urge ourselves – as if there were nothing of greater importance – to tell of how we spoke about her and even wrote about her then. There is always so much to be said. Hold back lest it overwhelm you, as the past sometimes does. Now that you are back on course, and the birds are light-skimming just above you in these woods which decline to a muddy and polluted basin of sorts – old car tyres, for example, wrenchings of iron as if at the hands of someone of near Herculean strength – there must surely arrive a moment of rest. Would he have lived hereabouts? you ask yourself as you watch the dust motes rise and then descend again in perfect order, the usual source of piecemeal enchantment. Would you say that it had all been reduced to shreddings? You are firm of step as usual, and I do envy you that, the way that you high-climb over the stoop as if no amount of lagoon water could ever o'erwhelm it. When were we there anyway, just the two of us, we contiguous coffins to come? Was that quite the right note to strike on a day as darkly glooming as that one? Bat it all away, dear simpleton. Imagine yourself as an earth worm, forever in a sober or sombre mood of restlessness.

When all the paper is laid flat, it will be evident at last who did all the work. There were always the shirkers, those who were contented to sleep through it all. And then there were the ones such as ourselves, high-wire acts all, or priceless pearls as we have often been called, *unsleeping guardians of probity*. Is that not how you would like to describe yourself? I did hear you say it once, but it is perfectly possible that you were muttering it over to yourself alone, testing it inwardly to see how it would fare once breezily out and about without a care in the world. Where we always must live, of course. No choice in the matter. Has a god made it so? You look for change to any of this, as if snapping your fingers and saying *hey presto concho!* would much avail. Sweetest pedlar of nonsense! I am frankly tired of looking. He is never there. Pardon, *she* is never there. What have you. We settled to the piano instead, a piece for four hands from the late nineteenth century, three of which may be mine, given that you have chosen to claim just the one. I look you over in some perplexity, register just how lop-sided you are these days since Hurricane Bernie whipped off the roof and deftly removed all but three of your teeth. Who could expect more in the wake of such a calamity? I agreed with you that I would remain calm. Calm as a clam is calm. Calm as a rock is calm. Calm as a tile skimmed down from a high roof is calm, the one which has lodged side-on in the soil of our kitchen garden. Like some terrible weapon. Calm now all the same. Do not give it grief, poor mite. A tile is defenceless when it is not on the move. Its role is to protect like any saviour of mankind anywhere. Sometimes you rise above your station, and then you are quickly brought down by the elements. Ditto I or me.

Such scheming days! They were always so hole-in-corner. That day when the beasts of burden turned on us, for example. I do remember it so well. As do you. I have still not cleared all the filth from my mouth...The bright sunlight, in which we always chose to walk (when we had the time and the space and the hours of leisure), is always to be trusted. Second only to nothing at all. Trust me to declare all this to you in my plummiest drawing-room voice. The steady lilt of this *new* voice of mine, on the other hand, together with its enveloping calm, and especially now that we have all made amends, will surely soothe you – in exchange for a matter of pence, I might add, somewhat jarringly, since you are sufficiently mean-spirited to be asking. I would not have insisted on it. No payment until all goods are delivered, checked, signed for. It is written on the side of the box. The usual perplexity, dumbwit? The old schoolroom at the very top of the hamlet, between the venerable bay and the enduring stench of the pig stye, always taught elementary reeling and writhing in my day, but then again, being younger, you are perhaps still forever lost in some mist of hopelessness – at least, that is how you have always pleaded every time that a pencil has fallen from your hand, and you have failed to extract it from between the floorboards. Anyway, to walk downhill is to reach a rapid conclusion of sorts, we are all agreed on that. There are no malevolent spikes up-jutting from the stony track by way of a warning – courtesy of some devil, of course. All that has been swept away. In fact, so much has been swept away which once left us feeling tired and disgruntled. Does this mean that we are on our way to paradise? By which I surely mean: have you tasted the dog food yet this morning, friend? Exactly. You must be somewhere hereabouts. I did not make a point of losing you. I have better things to do with my time. Count it, for example, second by second. A task to which I have just now set myself with no small degree of enthusiasm.

Here then is the truth of the matter. Why would I lie to you when it is I who am doing the paying? The toast is always buttered on the one side only. Where the dogs lead us, it is to those parts that we wend our way. I had not seen such scenery before, not in the course of those oh-so-abundant lifetimes that I have always so enjoyed. In fact, I had always believed myself to be set down in a landscape of black-walled factories, with all the smut and the smoke that is attendant upon such horror. Not at all! Not at all, geezer mine! That was all your yesterdays, came the voice in my ear, so pleasingly riddling, this morning. What is there to do about it then except to enjoy? I assent, with wild noddings of the head. I spring out of bed. My dog rises up to the full height of its hind legs beside me, secures the spiked leather collar around my neck, and then off we go, through brake and coppice, side-by-side running, with many whoopings and joyous shoutings! Is there any rest to be had? Will there be an end to such fervour? Lay your questions aside, you killjoys! Leave me to all my frantic exercises!

In such a state of dormancy, and still to be running pell-mell through the cabbage patch! That is what you always asked of me. You needed no less, you told me. And then you died, and there were other claims upon my attention, much of it appearing on rising ground beyond the outer limits of this township. The maleness of the male, and how it casts so many shadows. Would you discuss all this with me? Well then…There is never any real accounting for so much regret. We come and we go. Some of us remain, the hardier critturs. Forever on the lookout. We used to talk, during any idle moment (of which there were so many) of the shifting moods of clouds. Now we are at a loss to think much of anything else, having burned all the furniture. You were beside me when it happened. You even tried to spare two or three of the Windsor chairs. That is why the grunters came lumbering after you with flaming torches. There is never enough time to catch up with ourselves. You present yourself whole, entire, and perhaps even wholesome, but I envision you clothed top to toe in damp rags, still stinking of creosote. In short, a disgrace to the entire community of well-wishers, of whom there are so many, let me remind you. If you are not removed from here by Sunday, I may have to take the nature of predestination into my own rough hands.

Was there a light just then? Or did you conjure something special from flour, butter, yeast? I wouldn't put it past you. You always go beyond. I, on the other hand, always hold back. I scarcely even need to tell you that because you know me so well. Why do we even bother with each other these days? Why care about sticks and stones? Why lift God down from the shelf? These are all essential questions, I do recognise that fact, and sooner or later this rackety-heigh-ho life of mine will take an almighty swerve and bump into one or another of them. It happens like that. I have no illusions. I scarcely even possess a raincoat! They let themselves down, easy does it now, into the bitter darkness of the well. It was for hours that they were gone, I have no illusions. Then I began to despair somewhat. It crept up on me little by little like a wasting disease in which the skin begins to fall away. I was even beginning to imagine an entirely different future for myself. I saw myself running as far as the corner and then back again. You could even call it some kind of a miracle if you were desperate for a pleasing word, a word to soothe. And then it all happened as if it had never happened at all. They were standing there in front of me, frowning down at my shoes, my scuffed shoes. No improvement there, we all had to agree. I spent the entire evening in the cupboard, trying to piece it all together. None of it makes much sense to this day. No one has offered to pour concrete into the well.

In these times, things being as they are, I try to say as little as possible. I never know how many words are going to be available to me on any one particular day, so it means that I can let that conundrum go with a whoop and a skirl. There is no loss of dignity, of course. Worlds, everywhere hereabouts, are still in the making. I just wish that there were more to it than this, more admirable villages in the centre of France, for example, more novels by Zola and others as yet unread. I shall get to it all in time when my feet begin to improve somewhat. At least we still have that gleaming saddle to admire. Who chose not to throw away the polish? Such a happy accident of fate, almost Roman in its intensity. I never rode on the right. That could have been tantamount to staring into death's gaping maw. Bone-ugly. Your pose is admirable. No surprise that you still get so much work. I lie here on my side, languishing in the shadow of my own destiny. Do I exaggerate? Do I pretend to be something that I am not? What am I then? Do tell me. There could be a reward. From whose pocket? Do I hear you asking that? You have never lacked courage to scale the heights of insolence. I have always insisted on walking to the left of you in order to keep you from harm. If you were not an object of revulsion, you might have been my sister. No one would ever prevent you making such ridiculous claims.

At the costermonger's... Was that only yesterday, or am I engulfed once again by your dreams? I do wish that you would not impose upon me so. It is getting to be tiresome in the extreme. The coffee has been and gone. Thank you. Only so much, even if I have to say it again, and you can watch me if you wish to be indulged in the daylight hours, to which you have always laid such claim. I wish that I were you today. Don't be ridiculous. You have quite enough shirts in the wardrobe. Tantamount to a hurricane of fabric, and all so readily sniffable. I run as long as the breath enables, and then I stop because I have always been the sensible one, the one who can recognise a mismatched sock when he sees one. Speak for yourself. Your gestures, on the other hand, were always so clandestine, and especially when you sat on the upper deck of the bus, always going somewhere special. You carried your specialness with you just in case there were lean pickings at the terminus. You get my drift. Call me no better than a cloud. There could be a worse description. I could have taken umbrage, but I did not. I just let you drift away as if you were a sunshine holiday, scarcely to be believed at all. The wind carries me. Your words sustain me. Anything else you would like me to recall other than your face and how it shone beneath the moonlight? Remind me to replace these torch batteries. They are a source of such enmity when the human element is absent for a day or two longer than need be. Let me guess.

There were such crowds. I was reduced just then – never again – to such a condition of anxious anonymity. And then everything dispersed, and we were back at square one, cleaning the dominos on the table top with linseed oil, having just sold the cricket bat for a song or a sixpence, I forget which because it was all so long ago, hanging out there way back when in all my youthfulness. How it did shine! I tried to apologise just the once, and then I let it all go. I am who I am just as you are who you are, and that's about it. Needs must, babe. Don't forget to frolic in front of the glass. No one else will need to care. They do not even know you. Alas I do, and I shall, as long as you persist in harrying me along as if I were a hare or something. Goodness knows what. You do understand, do you not, that I am making all this up, in order to fill the day, which would otherwise be terribly empty, with cheesy thoughts of myself bearing down on an unlovely biscuit. That sort of thing.

What a surprise! They told me that they built the cathedral in a day and a half. It was pure accident that it had been sited at the end of the street, they added (having closely observed my knitted brow), tucked in just between the greengrocer's and the bijou coffee shop. We grew used to it. It was good for one's health to take the long way around it, adding at least one thousand steps to the four thousand or so. Eventually I discovered that it was making more of me than I had ever been, that I was rising up and up and up to match it. I was seeing beyond myself. I was even wearing different clothes – when I was wearing clothes at all. A few took exception to my unpredictable habits. They wanted me one regular height or nothing at all. I told them: ok, friends and you scattering of idle gawpers, I'll be nothing at all. Then I disappeared, never to return. The cathedral looked happy enough. It kept on dozing. An impish gargoyle scratched its balls. There is always some alternative to doing nothing at all. I didn't hear much about that until later though.

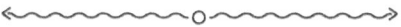

You say you try, and yet you do not try. At least I lift and then replace (say it after me, please), lift and then replace. That would be out there in the humped fields, when the countryside is roaring back into life. April, yes, when the juices begin to spurt. Mine, at least. I cannot accept that there will ever be an end to all of this telling because there is so much of you to be covered. I can never walk you end-to-end and then back again. You are inexhaustibly wearisome. You are also a closed door, and I do find that vexing. As soon as I am poised to walk through you, you slam yourself shut on me. I bounce back, of course, in the fulness of time, give or take a few salutary bruises. Nothing of all of this could ever be described as pretty. That is not the hand I was dealt. You, however, were indeedy the hand that I was dealt (I do accept that, with a degree of equanimity), and much else to fill the picture frame. I size. I square up. I run from time to time. I even sleep – there have to be interludes, or this way would lie madness. And then I wake up to it all again. Nothing has changed. The chair is here beside the bed. The spent matches are still lined up like so many victims beside the candle. The bread has not yet been baked. That tape of you is still playing. And still I cannot find it within myself to reach out and switch it off. It must be something which has bored deep inside, and then refused to leave. Ask yourself if you don't believe me... Somewhat. Grateful, I suppose, that you even asked. Many would not have, none of them known to me. Except you, of course.

It sticks. It always sticks. There can be no loosening up. The entire world these days is a sticking spot. Try it for yourself. Touch that door handle in the lobby, and you will never leave. It never used to be like this. Once everything was so fluid. We greased past and on. And then on a little further. There was no accounting for all that energy when we got going. And you too! I remember you up there in the air, lifting off and then landing, and then rising up again, weightless as the smallest single tear drop! Unfathomable matters known to us as sheer normality! Now it is all Not, Not, Not. The insupportable burden of each foot drag! Who could ever have guessed it? Who stepped in and said: no longer unencumbered! I try to deal with it as best I can. I have tried to minimise my life in order to avoid too much disappointment. I say very little. I use very few words, perhaps two or three at the most. I almost never look at you lest I should catch you looking back. No needless outpourings are to be risked. Almost anything would be way too much. You do understand why I am doing this, don't you? It's a pact then. As long as need be.

Did I hear you say something just then? Was that the voice I once knew? Has it been squeezed then – or worse? Are you being throttled? Is that why you seem to pipe and to squeal and to squeak when you turn and speak to me? Let us pause now for a little while before you try again. There is much here waiting to be looked at. You should divert yourself for an hour or two. Try that new painted, faux-antique street light, for example, and how it hangs pendant outside the window. You see — and it is so painful for me to tell you, you must surely understand — I don't want to hear it again. But if I do — if you force me by repeating it — I want everything else about you to be entirely different. Your face for example, and the way, having turned so gracefully on your heel, that your lovely neck used to look when you bent over the sink. I do not want any of that. You could even be something else — a beaten up cardboard box or a trash can or the corpse of a dog in the street, being picked apart by a raptor. All too disgusting for words. And yet somehow — and goodness knows how because I am not an evil man, I am only who I ever was and ever shall be — it would be a welcome alternative.

And then it all came down upon us again, as if it had never been away, all the pastnesses that we had never known, and had scarcely talked or thought or even heard about. And all at once too! Such deep foot-clingings of horse shit everywhere! Such a stench and such a clamour! With thousand upon thousand of them all coming on at us like an unstoppable wave, feeling their way with grasping hands, begging for a little relief, pleading for the least show of generosity. I just screamed, and then ran back to the upstairs bedroom where it was so quiet again, and I could pick up the toy soldiers from the tray, and keep them there for minutes on end, enfolded in my hot and trembling hands.

You told me more than once not to say it, and now it can never be unsaid, can it? It hangs there like a dead weight between us. Mine was not to give, you say. And yours not to receive? I retort with some bitterness. And so there is this landscape, which can do no harm in so far as it has been robbed of the powers of speech. And yet I do speak to it. I speak to it of you, you, incessantly. And, being partisan, it contrives to console me. It tells me that I am correct in every respect, and that you are the thorn which spikes my heel when I step back and lean against this rock, and that you are the wind, the chilling wind, which buffets me, and now, thanks to a chance onset of memory, you are also this sweet shaft of sunlight bearing down on me, momentarily.

Is this not what we might have expected all along, with the hall being as it is, so sun-struck, so unexpected this morning? Let us say that you walk out and try out a greeting on your tongue. For sheer bravura's sake! Or perhaps even two if there are two of us here. There may be. Anything is possible these days, you tell me. When you tell me anything, which is seldom. I do regret your absence almost as much as I used to regret your presence. Do you understand all of this? There is a measuring stick in the corner beside the wash stand. I am standing in the shadow of the painted metal shaft of a gas lamp, trying to measure up to all these days and parts of days – how finically diced they are today! – which are being thrown in my direction, willy nilly. I have not even begun to analyse the problem. It is too overwhelming for the very first hour of the morning when surges of optimism are said – by some. Who though? – to overwhelm us if we are paying too much attention. I seldom do. Pardon that irregular shaft of imbecility. Shall we now cut to the quick? A glass from the corner cupboard might help, cut glass that is, nothing morose or vulgar. Why heavy-hint at the general characteristics of almost all our neighbours? *Do right, and to you right shall be done.* Almost biblical, you might say. Or: another threshold to be crossed. More like my sort of contribution, Folksy, you could even say. If you knew me well. Can but try.

Lots of warm water slopped all over, as if to simulate Pharaoh's tragedy when he tried to cross over the sea and then at some point lost or found the bath plug. Am I confused all over again? Or was that your contribution to the debate? I wouldn't put it past you. You are knife-sharp when the wind lifts you. This is as much as there is to be said, wouldn't you agree? Silence is always the better part when sleet begins to ease off the edge of that cap with its ear muffs, the one I really love on winter days such as this one, those days when you hint at skiing and I prefer, as you might expect, to hunker down in the inglenook and stare at the rising flames, only *wishing* myself up there with the rest of them. Or the best of them? Which? I have no idea, old pal. You are the writer. I am merely looking on. Be assured, it is almost bound to happen sooner or later. That's the way things are. That's the way reality pans out. Yes it's all true, what you say, I do talk about it crudely and wishy-washily because I would never describe myself as a philosopher trapped in a barrel, though thousands have, several thousand I believe, and I have done nothing much to prevent it. Not so far anyway. In fact, some part of it quite appeals to me. The outdoors Johnny? That part? No, those ideas of darkness, sequestration and nausea even, when things begin to roll downhill at the speed of... oh my good no, just don't!

Is there much still left out there in the scullery? The report never mentions such things these days. And those little things contain, almost without asking, such a welter of meanings for me. I guess I am that kind of a person. No use turning my back on it. Sooner or later every man's scullery will catch up with him, and he will find himself lying back on the mattress, pulling out the torch, and then letting it begin to play across the surfaces of all those old, dusty things that some part of him had never failed to think about. So much hidden away! So much waiting to jump out! I don't know why. You tell me. You purport to know me. And if not, there is always the garden for a spot of errancy. This is where all that string must come in. Grandfather's inheritance. I am partial to string. It reminds me of all those beautiful musical instruments that I have never played. Really? You would? Well, I could spare one, but no more than that because I am so suspicious of your motives.

Shadow-boxing is what keeps me alive. It would keep anyone alive in a French village quite as somnolent as this one. Who lives here? Who ever lived here? And if there are by any chance those who live, do they ever eat? They don't come and go. No speech ever drifts up like so much chimney smoke into the ether, merely the nasty rip of a dog's bark on the air just in case you were ever thinking of venturing forth in that direction or this or that...Don't! Why lose a leg to unbridled appetite? I admire the cows at least. I would go out for them. I would make a habit of staring at their sleekly smooth brown flanks. Merely in order to see them standing there in that tight circle of theirs with their backs turned to us in such a clean gesture of contempt. They are such gentle mud-mashers! I do so love their contempt. You ask me why? The answer is that I do not return it because I am so grateful for their milk.

I believe that we would do better if there were more circles in the world. That thought came winging down to me as I stood beside the river, on an otherwise perfectly humdrum day, when I was up to my neck in calamity. Everything – the least little scratchy and vexatious thing, that is – seemed to fall away when I quietly, modestly rolled myself into a ball, and got someone to nudge me down the long incline and into the river. Each one of us manufactures his own heaven. Otherwise, it would be a matter of playing a game manufactured by others, the one that comes prepared and ready for use in a large black box with sheets of rules, and even a pair of gleaming compasses for accurately measuring out the pitch or the playground. I prefer to fling my arms about and let rip. The weather is my hero. It never seems to know what to do until it does it. I like that. As do you.

On that morning, you had shouted words that I have never to this day managed to understand, no matter how many languages you may choose to translate them into. You see – how shall I put it in order to make some sense? – one kite drifts off after another, as if there were always mindless games to be played, and always the same playmates with which to play them. I mean by that the kinds of kites used by children, reined in on a single long length of string, and so happy to be up there. And me with them on some days, when I can look down upon you serenely from afar, see you in context as it were. Your trajectory is always so interesting, the way you weave back and forth down the path to the shops, or arrow forth, so straight and determined. It all depends upon what hour it is, of course. Some day I let go of the string altogether. I bid it a fond adieu. I walk away. You don't even ask after it later. String has never quite managed to come between us.

Consequently I spoke a word or two, and those words had consequences. Some of them lodged in the mouths of others. Others resembled badly fitted, uprearing paving stones. Not that I could see them. They were in another city by then, and perhaps even in another country. How should I know? Why should I even care? We are all so carelessly carefree with words, and words want that to happen. They do not want to feel hemmed in or held back by any particular person. Would I? Would you? Well then.

We built it all together, but no one could *see* it, so no permission needed to be requested or granted. We were quite happy with that. It gave us scope to build faster and larger. All that building and building, on and on, took its toll on us. We each grew suspicious of the other because we could only ever *describe* what our respective contributions had been, and never exactly *see* them. There were other points of contention too. You thought that I had slacked and done next to nothing at the weekends, forgetting entirely that my mother was Jewish. I feared that you had built over a structure, one of my first, which had been particularly precious to me. There was no way of telling, of course. No, forgive me, that is not what I meant to say at all. There *were* ways of telling, and we used them all the time. The problem was that there was no way of telling that those ways of telling were truths or lies. You see, we never quite trusted each other. Why had we gone into business then? Whose life is in jeopardy?

Crossed wires in such strange circumstances. Not one but two, two, you always told me in your best and most vehement voice. I took it away immediately, explaining that some examination needed to be done. The problem was that the schoolroom was no more, and that memories were so completely undependable these days because memories feed on and build on memories, and there is nothing worse than that. What would happen, for example, if the foundations were rotten to the core? Do you have an answer to that one? I don't, but you could argue, perfectly plausibly, that I am only myself. The consequence of all of this was that we were hanging by a thread, and we knew it. You grew fatter. I grew thinner. We kept the curtains closed much longer than usual, and by the end we barely opened them at all. Finally, though, even that did not much matter because the darkness never went away. It just hung on and hung on because it knew that it needed to respond to the mood of any passing moment.

Paper comes and goes, they say. It lifts off with a jaunty, flappy wave. I don't like it to go. I need it to stay. I need much paper with me, for security's sake. Paper is padding. Paper is covering. Paper is a protective material. Paper thickens out when you lay one sheet down upon another. Even relatively thin paper can keep the sun off your face, though not the driving rain. Paper lets you down badly in the rain unless you have waxed it and waxed it for hours at a time, and that is a terrible effort I would not much recommend to anyone who values their sanity. Most of all though, paper is good for letting you know who you are and what you thought just then – or even what you are thinking now, right now, if you can write the words down fast enough. Words lie flat on paper and stare back at you, speak back at you. They remind you what your voice sounds like. They remind you what shape your thoughts are forming. Were you calm and collected or were you hysterical and aggrieved? They remind you who you are when you may chance to forget. They even remind you where you live if you are careful enough to write down your address. Which means that if you do not lose that piece of paper, you can return to a place you may once have confidently described as home.

Inching ahead, no more than that. Certainly not diseased any more. All disease has been left behind. The disease was winter enough. In fact, I have characterised *all* disease as winter now. Tall boots defined the legs. Mufflers disguised the largest of mouths. Even the cars, ubiquitous enough most days, desisted from parping. I liked it like that. Disease became our natural condition. You could even describe it as *spiritual* if you had some wish to take wing and fly. Some did, the venturesome, the lobotomised. We knew then that we were born to fade away, and now we could experience it even down to our finger tips. It was proving to be a delicious moment for almost all of us. Some disagreed, of course. The life-enhancers, for example, with their shellac nails. All green, needless to say.

If it refuses to happen, then *make* it happen. There's no other way. Well, the only other way is to stay still and become nothing at all. Would you be satisfied with such an outcome? Tintoretto, for example, he never stopped. If someone asked him for a *Day of Judgement* measuring, say, six metres by ten, his response, immediately, would be: what about twenty metres by thirty? Have you no space large enough? What's your budget, man? Then stretch it! Have you no idea of the significance of this event, and that it has taken sixteen hundred years to locate a Venetian like me capable of doing the subject justice? And he was not even that tall! I go my own way. I keep him tucked away at the back of the box like a talisman, or even in my mouth some days, a small, boiled sweet to suck on. It is not that in the sweet bye and bye I will *not* be preparing myself to do likewise. I may well do that. Why even hint at such a thing when you know how much bad blood has been spilled between us down the years? But until that hour comes, I have my old mother to think about, with her blue plastic crates stuffed full of old romance books. What should we do with them? That is the philosophical question of this passing moment. There is scarcely room for a bed any more. Someone will have to take the matter in hand, and there is no one here but me. Frankly.

<hr />

There were individual days and even entire historical epochs to to be dissected, and often quite intricately. We enjoyed all that. You could even say that we relaxed into it. All the murders, the maimings, the floodings of houses — and even the obliteration of entire estates when the storms swept through — we just had to deal with it all. And deal with it we did! No one could accuse us of being cowards. It was always only gaming, of course. That's how we coped with it, by calling it gaming. We even wore clothes for the occasion — you in that green hat to hint at the sudden, suspiciously early onset of spring in 1473, for example, when three quarters of a million — the roughest of guesstimates, of course — went down like skittles to the bubonic plague way up in the extreme, northern-most tip of Saxony. Did it hurt at all? Was it painful? Yes and no. We had developed this way of digging in and standing apart, the two things together, almost simultaneously. How did we do it? Call it a rare species of collective genius? Some have dismissed it out of hand. Some have called it callousness, a failure truly to engage with the enormity of it all, but I do not believe that to be fair. My palms are clean, front and back. Take a look. We were not evil. We were not even truly exceptional. Dogged, that would be my chosen word. Dog-like, in all my furious digging. Speaking for myself, for example, I was born at the back end of a piggery, in the most inconsequential of hamlets. Call it stinking back-alley country where almost anything went if you like. My father was a hand-fabricator of the commonest and most dispensable brand of clay pipes. My mother smashed rocks for a meagre living of sorts. How to account for my prodigious memory then, all those years of study spent at the University of Wittenberg? I was not even a ring leader in those days. There was no empire to speak of. It was all a ragbag, a mess. It needed to be sorted. One day when I was idling beside the well, musing upon the fluctuation of water levels, that insight hit me. Like a meteorite it fell. I rose to the occasion. And eventually I even dragged you up there with me.

This pathetic thing that I have here is not even a light to see by! It is just not dependable. Whenever I try to cup it between my palms, it flickers and then goes out, and I am left in darkness again. That's when all the questions begin to crowd in, aimlessly, from all directions, and also quite obsessively. Do we need light anyway, even this little light? Would it not be better to let our bodies and our brains grow accustomed to the darkness? Is there not even a light of sorts to be found within all this enveloping darkness? There are always too many questions1 Where did all these questions come from if there are always so few answers? There is just no point in them all turning up like this. Someone then has to provide for them, and even try to make them feel welcome. But they are not welcome. I believe that we should stop doing this altogether. We should banish all questions because with questions come acute anxieties about the fact that we never have the wherewithal to answer them. We feel badly about ourselves, as if we must always be inadequate. One tiny matter gets dealt with – the washer for this faucet, for example – and then, seconds later, the ceiling falls in, leaving you covered in dust and despair. Because the fact is that small solutions always seem to lead directly to very large questions. The questions never ever diminish in importance. They only grow and grow. Please don't ask me about myself. Let this suffice: I do not know why I do what I do. If I am a question, then, yes, I am an unanswerable question, one of those.

It was hick country thereabouts, as far as the eye could see. No better way to put it. And always too much of it. Always too much of *us*, any one of us. Superfluous. *De trop*. And the place itself so cloyingly viscous. Viscosity, that was my dream until I had to experience it, day by day, underfoot, and then I remember saying to myself: no way! So I left. And now I spend so much of my spare time, and all those times between times, thinking about it. It's a kind of haunting. I just can't seem to separate myself from all that I once was, even though I am not like that any more. The operation on the voice box saw to that. I'm squeaky-clean now. Hear me out, won't you? You don't have to leave just yet. There are chairs here. I bought two more yesterday in anticipation of a sudden surge in demand. And I do believe that it will come. This lull is the unnatural bit, all this waiting around for an audience whose nature is almost impossible to define until it is there, seated in front of you, with those giant boxes of popcorn on every knee, ever eager to listen. It has happened once or twice in the past. It will happen again. Life is a hula hoop, forever flashing by at the waist until somebody drops something and it all stops. Part of me would like to stop. Part of me would relish a slice or two of blankness, the falling away of all this anxiety, all this thinking, which is more like an itch than a thought, a maddening itch which never goes away, even when you go on holiday. Even the sea throws it back at you, all that you were, all that you can never escape being. Maybe I should be chipping away at something talismanic, in wood say.

It was yet another box to put things in. What are boxes for, goon? Well then. You brought it. At least I *said* you brought it because I most certainly did not put it there myself. I don't plant things on a doorstep on the understanding that someone will trip over them and perhaps even do themselves harm. I am not that kind of a person, So I was obliged, somewhat grudgingly, to bring it indoors, and even to open it because, well, there is no denying my insatiable curiosity. I can't help myself. I'm just built that way.

It had no bottom. Which means that something is likely to have fallen out. Let's investigate, I said to myself. There was no trail leading away from the doorstep, I checked that. Then I quickly realised that I had made a mistake – oh foolish man that I am! It had a glass bottom, so I could see through it to the cellar and all regions beyond. *Were* there regions beyond? I don't remember that at all. I thought it was just a plain cellar. This seemed not to be the case, so I climbed in – tight fit! – and then carefully examined the glass bottom. In fact, the left hand side of it opened outwards – by which I mean downwards, of course. Fortunately it was large enough – much larger than it looked – for me to be able to stand comfortably on the left hand side, lean down, and open it with the handle so conveniently provided. Having done that, I began to descend to the cellar. The steps were smoother and wider and much better made than I had ever remembered them. I remembered a flight of old, cold stone steps, and always so dangerously uneven. Not a bit of it! Could there even be underfloor heating down here? Impossible. Then I began to ask myself whether anything was really impossible these days. Later on, my perplexities only intensified. I became especially annoyed when my grandmother rose up out of her chair in front of the fire and *insisted* that I try on the christening gown.

You were only ever a part of me. Just as I was only ever a part of myself. We belonged to each other then. There were no two ways about it. Or about us. When I held your hand in mine, I felt as if your hand was my hand. Once you even walked away with my hand, claiming it to be yours. Did either of us get mad about any of this? Not at all! There was always such flexibility. Roads came and went. Some of them even stopped mid-flow, leaving the traffic stranded. Such ear-piercing screechings of brakes! I took a philosophical view of how things seemed to be turning out. What ever happened to the idea of destination? I asked when I reached – on foot – the junction of most contention. We all laughed to ourselves – I may even have laughed with you once – and then each went our separate ways. Birds may have been trilling above our heads. It was that sort of a day. Sometimes you would be on your own, and others would be crowding about you. The two things at once if you understand me. As if all the things that were, were also not. Do you understand any of this? Are you a part of this world by any chance? I am beyond all understanding now. My age has let go of me. It has abandoned me without a care in the world, My thoughts bid goodbye to themselves even before I have begun to consider them. Someone once described all this as sinister. They even suggested that I read a book. I call it jelly-like, being especially playful. I wrote one instead. This is it.

FINIS

www.ingramcontent.com/pod-product-compliance
Lightning Source LLC
Chambersburg PA
CBHW030039100526
44590CB00011B/259